YOU CAN ALWAYS

GET WHAT YOU WANT

Also by Phil Murray

Before the Beginning Is A Thought
Empowerment
The 49 Steps to a Bright Life
Bites on Personal Development
You And Me Make Three
Staying Awake Forever

YOU CAN ALWAYS GET WHAT YOU WANT

The Success Manual for Modern-Day Living

Phil Murray

Hodder & Stoughton

First published in 1993 by Perfect Words and Music
Published in 1998 by Hodder & Stoughton
A division of Hodder Headline PLC

10 9 8 7 6 5 4 3 2 1

British Library Cataloguing in Publication Data

Murray, Phil
You can always get what you want
1.Self-realization 2.Satisfaction
I.Title
158.1

ISBN 0 340 71789 0

Typeset by Hewer Text Ltd, Edinburgh
Printed and bound in Great Britain by
Mackays of Chatham PLC, Chatham, Kent

Hodder and Stoughton
A division of Hodder Headline PLC
338 Euston Road
London NW1 3BH

Dedicated to Ali, Luke and Eve . . .
with all my love

BEFORE WE BEGIN

The writing and researching of this book has been one of the most exciting experiences of my life. My discoveries have made a personal dream come true, and being able to share them with you is a bonus.

I always knew that there was more to life than was immediately apparent. I felt that if I looked hard enough, in all the right places, the big secret would jump out at me. It did.

The big secret had been no secret at all. Nobody had been hiding it from me . . . I had been concealing it from myself.

Way back in 1976, I had begun to set myself goals and targets, with *reasons for being* and purposes galore. I had big plans! I studied hard and worked late. I was nearly successful, but not quite. By 1984 I had embarked upon a path toward financial success, and departed my spiritual studies forever . . . or so I thought.

It wasn't until the second of January, 1993, that I had the realisation that really lit the fuse and launched the rocket. The bonus came in that my spiritual ideals were in no way compromised by my new strategy for success. In fact the exact reverse was true; I had more spiritual gain in my quest for riches than I ever had whilst *seeking the truth*.

In this book, I have outlined a route to success. You can travel this route, or you can seek out your own path. Either way, if you are successful, we will be utilising similar technology.

This is a starter package

I believe that you can be successful simply by utilising the technology contained in this volume, and marrying it to whatever is already within you, but I know that you will miss out on the slants and nuances of a thousand minds if you do not take your studies further.

In the bibliography at the end of the book you will find many of the works that I myself have studied . . . but some have been excluded. If I gained wisdom from a book, or gleaned some relevant datum from the writings of another whose intentions I did not believe to be completely wholesome, then I have not mentioned it.

So . . . don't fight it. Drop your defences, lower your guard, and follow me on a *mind-expanding experience*. Accompany me on a wealth-increasing mission, and set *no limits* to your achievement capabilities.

You can do it. I know you can, and what's more important . . . *You know you can.*

Have a good trip!

Phil Murray

WELCOME TO THE NEW EDITION

It works!

The technology and assistance contained in this volume has shown itself to be valid. Thank you for buying it, and welcome to the Path of Personal Development outlined herein. I have made additions since the first publication of the book, which are my own fine tunings to an already workable format.

I discovered the value of keeping a Mission Statement concise, and following through with a longer Visualisation Statement. This data has been added to the book. I reaffirmed my commitment to spiritual attainment as being the only true measure of *real success*. Such sentiment is more apparent in this edition.

People from all walks of life have benefited from *You Can Always Get What You Want*, and I just know that this new edition will further the good work.

The Positive Attitude Club, better known as the PAC, is no longer just an idea. It has matured into a concept that many others have made their own. We meet monthly in the modern workshop fashion for an evening of varied conversation and inspiration. I do hope that you will become a part of this group, or form one of your own. Either way, if I can be a part of your plans then that will be my good fortune.

I do not know of one good reason at all for hunger, war, or suffering of any description.

I see only solutions!

The problems of yesterday are the challenges of today, and human beings living in this New Age are discovering viewpoints that are up to the task we find ourselves engaged in . . .

Being successful and benefiting the whole of mankind!

I invite you to be an important participant in this challenge. I continue this sentiment in my book *Before The Beginning Is A Thought*. If you enjoy this work then I do hope you go on to be a part of *Before The Beginning*.

And now, before this beginning, let me welcome you on board a voyage of personal discovery . . . *may you never be the same again!*

With love and best wishes for your
own personal and interpersonal growth!

Phil Murray

CONTENTS

Stage One –
Are you ready for this? – page 1

a why you should buy this book
b how do you see yourself?
c the more you demand, the more you will get
d do you expect more from your life?
e junk
f forgiveness and Time To Myself

Stage Two –
The secret of self-esteem – page 19

g learning to like yourself
h Subconscious Mind and Conscious Mind
i talk to yourself and expect good results

Stage Three –
Whatever you can hold in your mind – page 39

j if you can think it and believe it will appear,
   it will
k visualisation and playing with the mind
l getting into action, the supergroup and
   1 + 1 = 3
m creating that picture just how you want it

Stage Four –
Money brings joy to the enlightened – page 59

n   it's easier being spiritual with
    a pound in your pocket
o   good reasons for borrowing and owning cash
p   copying the success of others

Stage Five –
Who is in charge now . . .
you or your mind? – page 73

q   fitness . . . positive attitude and
    a good strong purpose
r   determination is the common denominator
s   zipping and pinpointing

Stage Six –
Principle-centred, long-term goals – page 99

t   happiness is a by-product . . .
    choose your goals wisely
u   honesty, integrity and winning for all
v   the mission statement . . .
    long term versus the quick fix

Stage Seven –
Spread the word – page 133

w   good for you . . . good for others
x   where we all come from and the Big Picture
y   giving to others is like giving to yourself
z   living in harmony with the world . . .

About the PAC – page 143
Bibliography – page 147

STAGE ONE

Are you ready for this?

'*Begin with the end in mind*' Stephen R Covey

You must answer this question of readiness honestly if you are to get maximum benefits from your new life!

I want you to buy this book, and the chances are that you are browsing through the pages in some bookstore, looking for a good reason why you should part company with your hard-earned cash. If I don't hit you hard in the first few paragraphs, your money could go on something else. Okay, here goes . . .

I know the secret of success and you don't!

That is why you need this book. I can honestly say that if you are ready for lasting success, this book will provide the missing ingredients. I discovered this secret from someone else, who in turn discovered it from some of the most famous and successful people this world has ever known.

I hope that is a good enough reason to go and pay for the book. It is? Good!

To the business in hand. I want to present you with facts, as well as inspirational ideas. I have a duty to motivate you, but I am just the starter motor . . . the scope of your personal success will depend entirely on your dedication to being successful. You can't get success just through buying a book. You have to want it badly, then do something about it. You have to see it as the best option, then you have to pay the price that success will demand from you.

Lots of people know the secret of success. The secret contained *within* the secret is that the most significant ingredient lies within you, and success will not be forthcoming until you act upon the various elements of the equation without compromise.

I had been in the entertainment business all of my life. This does not lessen the validity of this material, nor does it mean that I am playing for the laughs, or trying for the tears as I sing the song. I believe that I have approached the field of human behavioural improvement from a sensible base, and have housed it in a very strong structure.

When I worked as a performer doing one-night stands – a baptism of fire for life itself – I was of the opinion that I should charge as much as the market would stand for my performance. I always said that if I had to make the effort to perform, it would be the same effort for a low fee as it would be for a high fee; I would perform for the same length of time. I always asked for the high fee, and I usually got it!

It's the same in life. You are going to be playing the game whether you like it or not. The same time is needed for a life of poor quality as is needed for a life of success. Perhaps this is not totally true as there is room to argue that you will allow yourself a longer life if it is to be pleasurable, but this part of the book is not the right place for that argument.

What I am saying is that you may as well concentrate on success.

Focus on the positive side of your personality

I had a partner for a time who felt that if we charged less for our performance we would get more work. I said that I didn't want to play the venues that couldn't pay the money, and suggested that we increase our fee while other artistes were decreasing theirs because of the recession. I wanted to position ourselves in the marketplace at a certain level.

Life is a marketplace and you have to position yourself in it. Are you a club singer, or cabaret? Do you write your own material, or use other people's? Do you give good value for money, or do you sneak off early? Are you chart material, or still waiting to get into the business? Do you record meaningful albums that will stand the test of time, or singles for the moment?

Will your new album still be played in sixty years time?

The same act can be seen in entirely different situations, and where that act is experienced bears as much responsibility for someone's opinion of that act as the quality of the act itself.

If I told you that I had written songs for the Beatles, or some other successful unit, you would be more inclined to listen to me than if I said that I was playing one-night stands in clubs and still had a day job. I'd have more trouble getting my message through to you, wouldn't I?

I always believe that the world is waiting for a Phil Murray song. Is your world waiting for you?

Other people have positioned you in the marketplace. Where have you placed yourself? If you positioned yourself higher, is that how you would be seen?

People usually reach their target. Did you know that what you are aiming for you will usually get? You have to ask yourself if you are aiming for the stars . . . and then answer honestly!

I had a guitarist who insisted that he was happy as long as he had his beer and cigarettes. Some of the band felt that he had a good attitude and was easily pleased. He was! I was relieved when he left the band because I felt that his expectations were too low . . . he never went without his beer and cigarettes, but those two things were all he ever got out of the band in which we were once both members.

The more you demand from your life, the more you will get out of it

Simple, isn't it?

If you are bored with the same old you, and think that there is nothing new and exciting lurking just around that corner, you are in for a surprise.

Are you tired of what you are, and think that there is no way of improvement? If the answer to that question is yes, then change your mind and brace yourself for lift-off!

I'm telling you right now that if you expect more from your life than you ever previously thought possible, you will get it.

Demand improvement!

You have bought this book so you must be after something more from your life. What I ask of you, is that as well as psyching yourself up with the positive affirmations contained in this material, as well as allowing me to psych you up with a short-term fix of well-being, as well as jumping up and down shouting yeah, yeah, yeah, with your pants around your ankles, and then rejoicing in the new experience of knowing that you can do anything that you want, you spare a thought for the future. Make a long-term commitment to yourself, for now and forever.

Commit yourself to a policy of continuous improvement for every aspect of your life!

Make that deal with yourself, and, as general as it is, your life can only get better. As your life improves in its various ways, your family and friends will not only notice a positive change in you, they will also experience a change in their own fortunes, which in turn will lead them to make efforts for their own self-improvement, which will of course reflect positively on you. So you see how easy it is to create a positive momentum, with you at the helm.

Endorse that policy now. *Continuous improvement for every aspect of your life!*

With every self-improvement programme you have to watch out for the Chinese meal syndrome. It is great while you are eating it, and for an hour or so afterwards, but it isn't long before you are empty again.

This one book is not going to be the end of your bid for a better life. It's a taster, a tempting morsel, an indication of what is on offer out there. You have to scout around and discover ways of bettering yourself that are relevant to you and your lifestyle. Different authors have styles that suit people in various ways.

I believe in the positive attitude movement

I believe that a positive attitude can surmount the insurmountable. I believe that you can move mountains. I believe that even the most miserable, snivelling, grovelling, creeping, failure of an excuse for a human being can be shown the way to success both as a person, and in life itself. Still, I do hope that not too many of you reading this right now fit that particular description, and if you do . . . good on you for recognising that a change is needed.

My style is to go for the jugular, an *'it's there so do it'* attitude. You will find gentler approaches . . . a velvet glove instead of my boxing glove. What I am saying is simply that the technology for self-improvement is out there and readily available, without a shadow of a doubt. Your own success is also already in existence and waiting to be accepted by you. So don't be put off by the carrier wave or the messenger. It's you that has to improve and change for the better ... not me that has to improve you. I will help, I may catalyse, but the ultimate responsibility is yours for ever.

I always wonder at people trying to give up habits they no longer require. Smoking is the obvious example, but the theory applies to any change you may wish to bring about. A friend of mine told me that he had just sampled nicotine patches, and they had worked as well as the hypnotist and the chewing gum that he had tried previously ... in other words not at all! I told him that they worked well enough, but it was him that wasn't working properly, expecting something else to do the job for him. He had expected magic, and didn't like the non-sympathetic approach that I offered him. He noted the sentiment however, and understood that ultimately the advice that I conveyed was sound.

I am not saying that I believe in the General Patton approach every time; but you must know that a world of difference exists between an aid, or something that helps you, and the actual decision by you to accomplish something. You can't ever blame an aid and also claim to be wholly responsible for yourself. You can search for better help, that is taking responsibility. It is your *response ability!* You must know that you are at the end of every line. When all the excuses are made, if the job has not been done, if the bed has not been made, the sale has not been closed, or the change has not been made for the better ... you are still there and there is no one else to blame.

Enjoy responsibility

This subject of responsibility is just too vast to be glossed over at great speed and in little depth. I am talking about the fact that you have to take responsibility for every single aspect of this universe, and the sooner you understand this principle, the easier your transition towards personal success will be.

After you get yourself into shape, you get yourself and your partner on an even keel and the kids feeling good about themselves; then you get your group of friends talking positively about each and every member of that group; then you move on to your town, your country, neighbouring territories, until you are in shape to look at planet earth . . . the universe. Can you can get this big a picture of things? You will! And why not try? It sure beats gossiping!

Surely a challenge of such magnitude is worth some effort. Can you appreciate the idea of total responsibility? Could you pick someone else's litter up? Could you serve someone without telling them? Is anything beneath you? Can you foresee a time when you will place £10,000 worth of used banknotes into an envelope and give it to your favourite charity? Will you outflow goodness anonymously?

Aspire towards being able to give away millions of pounds to good causes

A basic tenet of success is that outflow will always equal inflow . . . *and an altruistic attitude is a powerful magnet.*

I often wonder what would happen if our planet

were invaded. Would warring nations forget their differences? I know that they would. The differences between the West and the old Soviet Union paled into insignificance whilst the threat of Nazism hung in the air. As soon as the Nazis were beaten and the threat had dissipated, all the old reasons for hating each other resurfaced once more. It didn't have to be that way.

The Cold War came about because of a dismal web of mistrust and mismanaged communications between two superpowers. Lack of understanding and propaganda fed an existing fear of the unknown. Everyone focused on the differences of policy, and their own fear of change. How history would have been changed if the good points of both cultures had been embraced, and each side had focused on how they could help the other.

You have to be willing to move out of the comfort zone

You must respond to your circumstances with action and pure intent, based on honourable theory. You cannot become successful by remaining in your existing situation. This is your comfort zone, and it takes no effort to stay there. That is part of the recipe for stagnation – stay as you are; fear of the unknown; better the devil you know; best not try anything new . . .

C'mon now . . . you didn't buy this book just to remain in the comfort zone! Let us begin your journey by adding the ingredients of success to your life, and then see the difference when action is married to the principles!

Are you willing to do whatever is necessary to be successful?

If the answer that comes to mind is positive then I have a suggestion . . . if you hate anyone or anything, the only person who is harmed by that hate is you. The biggest and most valuable present you can give to yourself right now is the gift of forgiveness! To forgive every single person who you believe has committed a disservice to you would free up so much energy you would be amazed.

Begin by forgiving yourself!

Sounds crazy doesn't it? Forgive yourself for all the wrongs you have ever done to yourself and others. Do that right now! Let all the blame that is in you just float away, and introduce forgiveness. Don't regret anything that has happened in the past. You are going to start afresh, and before you can do that, you have to forgive yourself.

Forgive your parents

You don't have to tell them. No one need know. It's not a patronising act or a condescending thought. Just forgive them for whatever you think they did wrong. It is next to impossible to go through life without building up disagreements with the people you love the most. The very fact that you love them means that you will have been around them, or at least their viewpoints, more than people you perhaps like less. The chance of disagreement heightens as you grow older and begin to exert more self-determination. The transition between childhood and adolescence is fraught with difficulty. Parents are totally responsible for a child one minute, and apparently not needed the next. Parents had to learn too. They are not fully qualified until they have experienced every aspect of parenthood, and that is usually when the job of 'parenting' is complete and the necessary experience gained . . . too late!

Forgive your parents now and feel the relief immediately. Continue this process, and rid yourself of all the negativity that you have been needlessly carrying around. I know about all of those mental loops that can pop up, thoughts like . . . 'he doesn't deserve forgiveness' . . . 'why should I forgive her?' . . . 'they did it to me first.' Well, just forgive them for yourself.

Forgiveness is a selfish act

Give yourself this present. Award yourself this bonus. Forgiveness is also a big move towards getting what you want from life, and your own personal success.

You will need all of the attention units that are available to you for what lies ahead. You have to start creating habits that will benefit you. If you are ready for personal success, then you have to be able to prepare mentally for the future, and this takes mental prowess. Every single sentient person on the planet has the necessary power. Most people use the mental attention that is available to them on irrelevancies. We allow junk mail and junk ideas to impinge on our thoughts. We allow junk newspapers to indoctrinate the population with junk gossip. We turn on the TV to watch another unstimulating junk programme. We eat junk food and wonder why the health of the body declines. We swallow junk propaganda and buy junk.

Do you see yourself as junk? No? Then don't tolerate junk.

Don't feed on junk

The human mind is a great gift and needs to be treasured and used according to its design if you are to achieve power. If you fill your petrol tank with diesel, will it work properly? My job at this point in the book is to get you into a receptive state of mind to allow the technology of human improvement technique a sporting chance. Some of you will have filled your heads so full of circuits and bad data up to this point in your lives that perhaps you have lost the ability to look behind the headlines . . . you swallow whatever comes your way. If you have become complacent then I'm afraid you will just have to make an extra effort and push all that garbage to one side. We have to free up the mind, put it to work for us, and refuse to entertain any attitude that could work against a new future of total success. *Positive thinking is a habit that can be learned.*

I invite you to join the PAC – the Positive Attitude Club

As I am doing most of the work at the moment, I nominate myself Leader of the PAC. The only requirement for basic membership is commitment.

You then have to pledge allegiance to the idea that anything can be accomplished with a positive attitude, and until you do that you remain a Learner. Once you have made a commitment to the PAC pledge, then you become a Practitioner. With an accumulation of relevant knowledge, you will become an Advanced PAC Practitioner.

The aim of this book is to set you on course to full achievement

As a Practitioner, you make a further pledge *to change something for the better every day*. This is a process that begins within. You must continually eliminate negativity from your thought patterns. Don't worry . . . help is available! There are many people now writing about the subject of personal awareness, and you will also be helped throughout this book by me. This help will only be apparent if you are a Practitioner. The Learners have still not taken the plunge, and will need to pledge allegiance before the benefits of club membership can be bestowed upon them. The PAC is both a concept that you can carry in your mind wherever you may go, and a physical actuality. The PAC is a way of being and an art of living; it is a love of life and people, an oath of awareness, and a symbol of your beingness. The PAC means commitment to a future of interdependence, joy, happiness, prosperity and achievement. The PAC exists wherever these attributes live . . . and they are all within you! If they are dormant, then begin to use them and celebrate their rediscovery. If you already know them, then reconfirm your love of them. Let us celebrate the PAC concept!

PAC members are entitled to improve their lives and well-being

As you read this book, you will realise more and more that it essentially deals with the mental aspects of preparing you to achieve success. The physical action necessary to realise your full potential is vitally important, yet I leave that aspect mostly to your own inner knowingness.

At no point has the fact escaped me that success can appear in many guises. *I also know that you all have different definitions of success.* You will soon realise that even if your sole purpose for reading this book is to get rich, then a by-product of that wealth will be spiritual gain. Conversely, if your main objective is spiritual gain, perhaps you will see the value of great wealth as we proceed.

If you decide that you would like to sail the Atlantic, you will need to train hard and organise yourself well. You will need to prepare your body for the constant motion. The boat will need attention, perhaps even an overhaul. Your mind will have to be tuned in to the challenge. That is what I am doing with you right now. We are talking about forgiveness, and that is one thing that can give us a quick fix, a boost forward, a thrust from the engine . . . it can free up those attention units that, as Practitioners, we have decided we need in order to progress at full speed ahead.

I believe in this quick fix!

Forgiveness has been on the agenda forever. Just think of all the preachers and prophets who extolled the virtues of this simple little act throughout the ages.

Do you think they talked about it for fun, or because it didn't work? It is a soul-cleansing activity. A hurdle to freedom. Jump it and see what is on the other side!

When was the last time you emptied your head? This can take a lot of practice, and I truly believe that some people go through life without ever being alone with themselves. Some call it meditation and some don't have a word for it because they can't conceive of the concept. *I just call it Time To Myself, or TTM.*

Great songs and ideas come to me during this TTM. I can solve the problems of the world during this TTM. It's a quality of life to me that I now could not be without. *You have to make it happen.* Those times when you say that you are too busy . . . they are just the times you will discover TTM to be most efficacious.

Find a space where you can truly experience TTM. The top of a high mountain, or the middle of the Pacific Ocean on a luxury yacht would be ideal. Given that these ideals are perhaps unrealistic and impractical, try parking your car in a peaceful place, somewhere away from distractions, preferably in an aesthetic environment. You may be fortunate enough to have a quiet room in your house. The location is for you to find. When you are practising TTM, you are not doing anything else. You are not thinking. That would be TFT, or Time For Thinking. You are not listening, watching, eating, smoking, drinking or shuffling around in a chair.

Your ultimate goal is to get out of yourself or exteriorise . . . to be aware of your ability to control your mind and body. We will talk later of the different parts of the human being. Knowing about this will be a major benefit, but it comes later. For now, we will aim for a peaceful environment without conscious thought. If solutions to problems appear for you, then fine. That is the subconscious mind working for you.

This TTM will eventually become the idea generator of your new lifestyle, and will provide you with many answers to those problems that we both know are going to crop up from time to time. Treat TTM as essential, and not a luxury. You will discover a peaceful side to yourself amidst the hustle and bustle of the modern world.

When it is impractical to achieve true TTM, then you must create a space in your head to which you can retreat and recharge the batteries. I had a wonderful time in the Florida Keys one year, and I have one particular picture to which I retreat when I feel a little overwhelmed. I was with my wife and two children; we had just driven down from St Petersburg on our way to Key West, when we stopped on one of the first few Keys for a break. We believed that we had found paradise. There was clean sand bordering the blue sea, hardly anyone around, and a stillness and serenity that you don't often find in holiday destinations. We looked out to a headland. The sun shone, and there was a lone palm tree gently swaying in the warm breeze.

I spent my childhood looking out on to the banks of the River Tyne in the north east of England. It is easy to see why such a panorama had this kind of exhilarating effect on me.

The point is that I use this picture and experience as a sanctuary. If I am worried about some kind of deadline, an upset in the family, or the cheque that has not arrived, I just *go to Florida*. This isn't running away. It is an intelligent use of the facilities at my disposal.

A friend of ours used to tell us that not a day went by without her worrying about the world and its problems. Boy, if you want to give yourself a sticky time, think about that imponderable. There is no point whatsoever in worrying about the world. This friend of ours could have come to Florida with us. In our paradise, with a little TTM, we could have thought up one answer to one problem, acted on it, and done more for the world than the average town does in a year. Worrying is not creative . . . the stillness and solitude of TTM is!

Great ideas-people throughout the ages have used TTM to realise their place in history. Great inventions have been created with TTM, a pencil and some paper. People have earned their living by 'sitting for ideas', using TTM. This literally meant that they would sit in quiet solitude, and allow their subconscious minds to present them with solutions to problems.

So, we have touched on some valuable points in this first stage of your accelerated journey to personal success and fulfilment, and I think you are ready for the next stage. If you have joined the PAC and have begun to take responsibility for yourself and others, tackled the subject of forgiveness, and experienced TTM, then I think you are ready for *the secret of self-esteem* . . .

STAGE TWO

The secret of self-esteem

'The more you like yourself, the less you fear failure and rejection' Brian Tracy

You have to like yourself before you can expect other people to like you

I'm not talking about the big-headed, empty vessel, vane type of liking yourself. I'm talking about the real thing, *a genuine liking of the genuine article . . . You!*

For this to occur, you have to understand just how unique you are. There is no one walking this earth today who is the same as you. For this reason alone you are special. And if you add all the good ingredients that you know are inside you to this original and unique being . . . do you begin to see that liking yourself is possible? Well I'm here to tell you that it is more than possible, it is pleasurable and essential.

My father used to look in the mirror every day and say to whoever was within range, *'How would you like to be as good-looking as me?'* He exuded confidence, and of course I, like many boys with their fathers, aspired to be just like him.

Occasionally, we would have visitors who would sometimes comment that my father seemed big-headed and selfish . . . but he wasn't! He just knew that he was good-looking, and didn't mind being demonstrative of that attribute. He could have been ugly, but if he had looked in the mirror every day and commented on his good-looks, then you can bet your life he would have felt good-looking, and that feeling would have transmitted itself to others.

That reminds me of the famous story about the early days of the motor car, and while we are on the subject I have to mention that I had planned to exclude any stories about Henry Ford from this book ... along with Colonel Sanders, Coca Cola, Andrew Carnegie, McDonalds, Wrigleys, Woolworth, J C Penney, any American President or British Prime Minister, Emerson, Edison or Einstein. However, this is not possible ... nor is it fair. For a while, I felt that the Americans were stealing an unfair lead in this race for human behavioural improvement and I wanted to shout out for the British way.

The stories of success were just so readily available from across the Atlantic. It was in the United States that Andrew Carnegie offered Napoleon Hill the job of interviewing a massive amount of well known millionaires, to discover the common denominators in their success stories. Carnegie himself was a Scotsman. He was revered, respected, and extremely wealthy. It was Carnegie who furnished Hill with letters of introduction. Without these letters, Hill would not have gained an audience with many of the millionaires that he needed to interview in order to complete his assignment.

For me to have kept this book totally British, I would have needed letters of introduction from a figure such as the Duke of Edinburgh, to Anita Roddick, Richard Branson, Alan Sugar, Eddie Shah, Clive Sinclair, Andrew Lloyd Webber, Paul McCartney, George Harrison, Ringo Starr, Mickie Most, Elton John, Dennis Thatcher and perhaps even the Queen. I felt that these people were the modern Great British counterparts of the politicians, industrialists and inventors that Hill had interviewed all those years ago. It was not my goal to do that in this book, but I think it is an excellent idea for the future.

Anyway, back to the story . . . the fledgling American car industry used to close down for the winter. People reckoned that you had to garage your car to protect it from the bad weather. This attitude reflected on sales, which remained stagnant . . . as slow as a trickle. Year after year, it was noted that this trickle came from the same garage out in the Mid-West. Henry Ford sent a top executive to find out why this dealership was selling cars in the winter, against the trend. The executive asked the owner, and the owner said that *he didn't know that you couldn't sell in the winter*.

The owner of the garage saw no reason for not selling his cars during any season. If he had told himself that sales were not possible at this time of year, or gone into agreement with his fellow garage owners, the sales would not have occurred. *If you tell yourself that you like yourself, this liking of yourself will begin to help you.*

The indoctrination of true self-esteem is an aid to positive progress!

Compared to the louder American culture which seems to bare all, we British show an apparent passive humility. We don't like to shout about our good points too loudly lest someone hears! The class system still seems to be in place, and we still feel an obligation to behave in certain prescribed fashions if we are to be accepted by those in a particular social stratum. We are aware of vulgarity, and use the word to describe newly acquired riches, which are often categorised as unrefined and very much inferior to *old money*.

Along with self-esteem, saying good things about oneself and others, taking positive viewpoints, and having honourable and burning ambitions, the theory of simple success needs to be embraced and studied. Insincere humility will act like a brake to your onward progress . . . disregard it, banish it, and favour ability, honesty and integrity!

The world is constantly changing, and we run the risk of being left behind unless we begin to embrace the modern viewpoints that are helping other cultures to make giant leaps forward. The Japanese have a fabulous outlook on industry. Many of the top firms in Japan treat employees as family.

I was interested to follow the progress of Nissan, when they began manufacturing in their brand new car plant in my native north east of England. This was an area that had prospered through the boom of the shipbuilding era, and floundered when it could no longer stay competitive in the world market. The men were used to striking when a little more dialogue could have kept them working. The bosses were used to throwing their weight around, without a care for the struggle and plight of the working man. The good news is that the customised Nissan way is working here in England, even though the general world recession has justified certain job losses. Mixing new ideas with an understanding of our own ways can work a little magic!

A successful future belongs to the modern alchemist . . . an ability to mix and match ideas, a combination of risk and profit, sampling new ways, invention, the nurturing of all kingdoms, mineral, animal, human

and spiritual, creativity, the love of mankind in all
that you contemplate and achieve!

We can work a little magic together . . . with this
book, the future, and your intrinsic ingredients. You
must discard the old habits that have not been fruitful
in favour of the new chemistry of the now. The concepts
described in this book are tried and tested . . . they are
available to you as you assimilate each and every one
of them.

Along with the New Age and the New Millennium,
new outlooks will increasingly permeate the old working environment. Boss and worker will synergise into
a New Age relationship. These attitudes will percolate
through into all industries. We must be willing to
embrace ideas from alien cultures if we are to prosper
in the new world market. We have to bolster our
plans, preen our feathers, strut our stuff, shout out
our attributes and tell the world that we like ourselves
again! We will then, once again, be ready to play the
game as major competitors.

You have to like the mistakes you have made

The mistakes have got you this far in life along with
all the good moves. It is often the mistake that spawns
the success. Learn from your mistakes. Treat them as
an essential part of the lesson. Like and see the funny
side of all those thoughts that you dread anyone ever
finding out about. Enjoy the clumsiness, and appreciate
the time you broke your favourite cup. There is no point
whatsoever in hating anything at all, and no space for
embarrassment in anyone's life. Inability to confront
anything is a serious liability. If you have the choice
between liking and hating, you may as well like.

People who like themselves are very attractive

Did you think that liking yourself was a no-go area? Are you so accustomed to self-criticism that you won't allow change? It's a funny thing, but as soon as you begin liking something, no matter how negative that thing or thought or person may be, its charge of negativity begins to dissipate. Feel the pain disappear from an unpleasant memory as soon as you see something good in that recollection.

You are now going to change any useless internal dialogue that goes on inside your head for something more beneficial. It could be an unpleasant picture in your head, of a time when you fell to the ground from a swing and banged your head . . . yes, you remember the pain, the embarrassment, the bruise, having to stay off school the day you were due to play on the football team for the first time . . . you just have to find the good in that picture.

Before you say there can't be any good in such a painful memory . . . was the sun shining? It was. You remember the warmth on your cheek. And now you remember how kind all of your friends were to you, and the sweet smell of freshly mown grass. *Good*. This works with any mental picture of whatever content. What would you rather focus on, the pleasure or the pain? Find the good in the pain, and no matter how small that good is . . . find . . . focus . . . feel.

Perceive a mental picture as you wish it to be . . . not as it has been imposed

Maybe this concept of recording pictures in your brain is new to you. The fact that you are making a high quality movie of every single frame of your life from birth and before, to now, is an actuality whether you acknowledge it or not. But this kind of movie is different. It has not been seen in the cinema . . . yet! This movie contains smell, emotion, taste, likes and dislikes, decision and indecision.

Even better than all that, you can edit this movie and get it to show just as you want it. *Special, eh?*

We can quickly perform a little exercise here to illustrate the point. We need to use something that we all know about and can relate to in some way, shape or form. I've got it . . . I want you to get a picture in your mind of a cow. Read this paragraph over a few times to familiarise yourself with what you have to do, then close your eyes and make that picture of a cow appear in your mind. Do you see that picture? Good, you see it. Make it a black and white cow, and have it stand in a green field, all alone, chewing on some grass. Got it? The sky is blue and the sun is shining. Make the cow lie down. Make it get up. Now make it sing and dance. Do this a few times, have a laugh watching the cow dance, and then make it disappear.

The first thing I want you to ask yourself, is who made that picture? *You made that picture.* Where was the picture? *It was in your mind.* Good, you placed that picture in your mind. Where is your mind? *In your head.* Could be. The head that makes up part of your body. I want you to understand right now that . . .

You are not your body.

You are not your mind.

You are you . . . a spiritual being with many abilities and qualities quite unrelated to the mind and body!

You use the brain to manifest a mental picture of what you, the being, perceive, and you call this your mind. You house your mind in the brain, and the brain in your body. Then you try and forget the differences between you, your mind and your body, and you, the mind and the brain.

New babies should arrive with manuals! Can you imagine trying to work out a new computer software package without the instructions? Well, that is what we have to do if we are to fulfil our true worth on this planet. We can begin by discovering a workable formula for liking ourselves.

If you have a different viewpoint on the subject of human beings, and that outlook is working for you, then unless you are in the business of studying the psyche, stick with it. If you like the sound of my viewpoint then embrace it, and see if it works for you. Life is more fun as a spiritual being, and I have known forever that I am exactly that. I have experienced past lives in detail. I have known other planets and different forms of communication. I have experienced birth and death more times than would be possible to relate here in these pages.

More important is the fact that I am now discovering more and more people, with each day that passes, who also know this postulate to be fact.

I have reached a point where I know that I am in command of my mind at any given time. I am in control. I cannot imagine a worse punishment than going through life thinking of myself as a 'meat' body. I would then have to embrace the viewpoint of an animal. I would merely strive to survive. But as a being playing the body game, a whole new philosophy comes into play . . . and there is no unfathomable mystery to it!

I know of some religions, sects or cults that take an

eternity to unravel these secrets. They say that you have to do this, that and then the other, give levels of realisation fancy names, and charge a zillion just to allow you on the first rung of their ladder, which they tell you is only to be climbed by the chosen few.

I have news for you. You can start as high up the ladder as you wish. If you feel that your mind is sometimes in control of you, then you can try some commands that make you pop out on top again. Become a PAC Practitioner and use TTM. Try visiting my paradise or discover your own. Try telling yourself to step out of your mind. Command yourself to govern. Be aggressive if need be. Do whatever is necessary to remain in control at all times. Feeling good about anything ensures that you have more substantial abilities at your disposal than might otherwise be the case. There is no doubt about the fact that you can achieve far more in life as a happy person than you can as a miserable pessimist. Philanthropy is senior to misanthropy. Altruism is more beautiful than egoism, and the first step towards this quality is a healthy love of yourself!

Have you ever heard about self-talk?

That's right . . . talking to yourself. People used to be locked away in mental institutions for doing just that. Now you can buy books on the high street about that subject alone. Many authors have written about the power of self-talk. Some have turned it into an art form.

Did you know that your subconscious mind cannot tell the difference between fantasy and fact . . . *you can literally fool yourself to success*? Whatever you tell your subconscious mind, it will believe and act upon. If you tell it that you like yourself, then it will consider this to be true. If you tell it that you are successful, then it will do everything in its power to turn that positive success suggestion into a physical reality. If you tell it that you are stupid, then it will help prove you correct. This last paragraph is of such staggering importance, that I would like you to stop reading for a while and just think about it.

Mental success precedes its physical counterpart!

I spent a portion of my life erasing stressful times from my memory, of this lifetime and others, and this was beneficial to a degree. Even though it involved focusing on the negative, the action of facing up to a previously unconfrontable memory released attention units for positive use elsewhere.

I misunderstood the subconscious mind, thinking that it only harboured negative things, and I spent all of my time trying to erase them. When I occasionally succeeded I felt relief, but I wasted the effort by not commanding my subconscious mind to do anything positive for me using the released energy from the erased pictures. I just treated the subconscious mind like some kind of negative presence. Now I know the truth, and sharing it with you is as exciting for me as first discovering it for myself.

The subconscious mind is the most powerful computer in the world. It does exactly as it is told. It works in the present tense and always as if it is, and you are, exactly as you have suggested.

Oh boy, if only I had known this fact a few years

earlier. Now you can really get into the serious, yet fun, business of powerful personal change! What are you going to do with this secret of wisdom that the world has withheld from you for so long? How are you going to harness the awesome power of the most formidable power centre ever conceived? We all have one. What are you going to do with yours?

You must know that this subconscious mind, or SM, is very different from your conscious mind, or CM. You use your CM to run your everyday life. You can hold one thought at a time in the CM. The CM has a fraction of the power that is contained in the SM. The SM is labouring steadily, every minute of your life, serving you as it has been commanded. It is the SM that will give you inspiration, or sudden solutions to problems. This can often happen during TTM. Sometimes it will answer your question after you have forgotten what that question was. The SM likes time to work on your commands at its leisure. How many times have you had a name on the tip of your tongue, and an hour later it has come to you? That is the SM at work, constantly striving for success.

I picture my SM as a giant office with a huge storeroom full of files. I have an archive section, a microfilm section, a memory chip section, a pending section, and a section for continuous action. Audio, visual, film, the feel department . . . this marvel has everything I need for success and it is a beautiful place. There are computers everywhere and a large staff of very contented friends.

My best friend in the office is my secretary. When I want something from the SM, my secretary always gets it for me. I have a Messenger, and I use my Messenger to send messages to people and places. I have a Guardian, who ensures that I am safe and sound at all times. My Guardian sometimes uses my

Messenger and vice versa. They both have access to my secretary. They all trust each other and I believe in them implicitly. They are all my best friends. We are interdependent! I have deep faith in my SM and I treat my helpers there with utmost respect.

You must understand that I am not talking about any kind of surreal magic when I say that the SM will get you into situations that are exactly right for what you want in life. The SM can see things that the CM cannot. Hunches are given to you routinely by the SM. You can bet your life that for every hunch you are lucky enough to be given by your SM, it has worked overtime to retrieve or conceive of it for you. Your secretary may have scoured millions of files, your Messenger could have journeyed on countless missions, and your Guardian would have been watching over these events all the while.

Consider this. You are looking for a special type of guitar for the new band that you have just joined. It's a pedal steel and you have never been interested in such an instrument before. Next thing you know you are at a gig and there is a country band playing. You talk in the dressing room afterwards and it transpires that the pedal steel player is just about to upgrade his guitar as he has just inherited some money. You buy the guitar that you had decided on there and then.

Now perhaps you were looking in the window of some newsagent or other, and this gig may have been advertised there. You were not really interested in country music gigs as you were looking to buy a kettle at the time. In fact, you probably didn't consciously see the advert at all. Your SM did though. It also noticed that the guitar player was selling his pedal steel. That was a separate advert. The SM linked them for you and suggested you go to the gig. The SM gave you the desire to attend a potentially beneficial event. It used this data, gathered from a newsagent's window, in its search for a possible answer to your desire. To that degree the SM is magic as we know it. When you also consider your telepathic abilities, which we will discuss later, the fact that you could just attract the right situation by sending the SM a light thought concerning your requirements . . . well, we can call it magic-magic if you wish.

I can help you programme the SM

Together we can begin by filling the SM so full of your present dreams and aspirations, that if you persist and work hard at implementing this rediscovered technology which is now available to you, I guarantee your life will change for the better within twenty-one days. Are you ready for this part of the formula? Are you prepared to tread this path and reap the rewards?

The secret of self-esteem is in knowing how to inject yourself with as much of it as possible

A very workable way of giving yourself this essential injection is to record yourself a cassette tape of personalised affirmations. Play your favourite relaxing music in the background, as this seems to open the mind to your positive suggestions. A feeling of deep relaxation is also an aid to the absorption of new data.

This is what I want you to do right now. Read

through my list of positive affirmations (pp. 34–37). If
my words are good for you, then that will give you a
quick start. Read them out aloud. Sing them. Have a bit
of fun with them . . . but be serious about the desired
outcome. Look in the mirror and get affectionately
acquainted with yourself. You are about to change
your life for the better.

Put your favourite music on at a relaxing volume

The music should be instrumental only. I enjoy Bach's
Concerto Number One for the violin in A minor. I
climb with the crescendos, relax into the atmosphere,
and emphasise my affirmations in a different way
each time. I also feel good with soothing music,
and find that it is just as beneficial as it drifts
by me.

On my Audio Cassette Success Programme, I have
had some new music composed especially for that programme, which has been tested with my affirmations
and found to be just as expeditious as the classics.
The combination works well for me. This music and
these affirmations were written for a general purpose,
however, and I recommend the customisation of them.
If you can get hold of this Audio Programme it will
help you understand the practice and theory of self-
talk. You may wish to make your tape more subliminal,
that is, have the affirmations just too low for the CM
to hear comfortably. I prefer to hear exactly what
is being said, however . . . I enjoy being in total
control over as much of my life as possible. We
let enough unwanted data slip into the SM as we
inadvertently suspend awareness and stroll through

life, without relinquishing control when there is no necessity.

If you feel at ease with this concept, which certainly works well and is definitely easy to accomplish, then I expect you to make up your own programme of personalised affirmations with your favourite music in the background. You can increase and decrease the volume as it suits you. You could even write and record your own music if you are that way inclined. The object is to get as much of *you* into this programme as possible.

For now, relax and listen to some music whilst reciting and emphasising my list of positive affirmations. This will familiarise you with the philosophy, and get you accustomed to the type of things to say, sing, or chant.

Once you have mastered any inhibitions you may have, get yourself a cassette recorder and have some fun recording your own voice, with your favourite music playing in the background. Get used to hearing yourself. I know this is hard to begin with. I had to do it for the first time, too. Now I love using my voice for affirmations. I enjoy hearing what I have to say, because *I always tell myself good things*.

This is not hypnosis. This is communicating with your subconscious mind. You are suggesting an internal dialogue for the future. If dialogue is necessary in your head, then you should be in control of it. Every communication must be in the present tense. I'll use the first person singular to begin with, and then the second person singular for additional benefit. We use the first person, as that is the way we have grown used to inadvertently talking to ourselves. We are, however, also accustomed to being told by others that we are a certain way, hence the additional use of the second person. Always talk to yourself with the idea that what you want, or how you want to be, is already accomplished.

Let's walk the talk

I call this part of the programme *affirmations . . . talk to yourself and expect good results.*

1. I like myself, I like myself, I like myself.
2. Life is good and getting better all the time.
3. I am a good person.
4. I enjoy my family.
5. I am clever.
6. I am wise and hold my own counsel.
7. I have a healthy body.
8. I am the perfect weight for my height and build.
9. I am honourable.
10. Integrity is an important part of my life.
11. I have a healthy way of living.
12. I am tolerant and interested in other points of view.
13. I am a good learner.
14. I feel in harmony with my surroundings.
15. I am in harmony with the world.
16. I have a good sense of humour.
17. I enjoy listening to people.
18. I am in control of my mind.
19. I feel powerful.
20. I am willing to change a decision for a better viewpoint.
21. I love my family.
22. I am a creative person.
23. I see my life in long-term vision.
24. I always have excess money to give away.

25. I enjoy giving to others.
26. I always go the extra mile.
27. I give over and above what is required of me.
28. Money seems to be attracted to me.
29. I enjoy a feeling of inverse paranoia.
30. The world is conspiring to do me good.
31. Good things always seem to come my way.
32. People just seem to like me.
33. I am thought of as being good company.
34. I always seem to do the right thing.
35. I am gifted with determination.
36. I always get what I want and others benefit along the way.
37. I enjoy working towards the achievement of my goals.
38. I like helping others.
39. I learn something new every day.
40. I am a high achiever.
41. When I win, my family and friends win also.
42. I am happy with myself.
43. I am happy with the world.
44. I enjoy my own company as well as other people's.

1. You like yourself, you like yourself, you like yourself.
2. Life is good and getting better all the time.
3. You are a good person.
4. You enjoy your family.
5. You are clever.
6. You are wise and hold your own counsel.
7. You have a healthy body.
8. You are the perfect weight for your height and build.
9. You are honourable.
10. Integrity is an important part of your life.

11. You have a healthy way of living.
12. You are tolerant and interested in other points of view.
13. You are a good learner.
14. You feel in harmony with your surroundings.
15. You are in harmony with the world.
16. You have a good sense of humour.
17. You enjoy listening to people.
18. You are in control of your mind.
19. You feel powerful.
20. You are willing to change to a better viewpoint.
21. You love your family.
22. You are a creative person.
23. You see your life in long-term vision.
24. You always have excess money to give away.
25. You enjoy giving to others.
26. You always go the extra mile.
27. You give over and above what is required of you.
28. Money seems to be attracted to you.
29. You enjoy a feeling of inverse paranoia.
30. The world is conspiring to do you good.
31. Good things always seem to come your way.
32. People just seem to like you.
33. You are thought of as being good company.
34. You always seem to do the right thing.
35. You are gifted with determination.
36. You always get what you want and others benefit too.
37. You enjoy working towards the achievement of your goals.
38. You like helping others.
39. You learn something new every day.
40. You are a high achiever.
41. When you win, your family and friends win also.

42. You are happy with yourself.
43. You are happy with the world.
44. You enjoy your own company as well as other people's.

What do you think then? Did you feel clumsy, awkward or even stupid? Maybe you enjoyed the experience? Perhaps you felt a little nervous anticipation? A mixture of feelings? You should know that this experience is beneficial . . . and this alone should allow you to continue with the exercise each day, until you feel totally at ease with the technology and begin to see some promising change!

I advise you to work on your affirmations continuously. Master the wording of them and enjoy the rhythm. I have achieved a state of automatic optimism through affirmations, and I accent happiness, cheerfulness and readiness for life . . . states that have all been helped and enhanced through affirmations.

When I began utilising the technology of personal affirmations, dark old ways would impinge whenever I chanced to drop my guard. This does not happen any more because of commitment. My frame of mind is exactly as I want it – *dynamic, and positively charged*. I have my own data in the SM and it is working for me. As Leader of the PAC, I have progressed speedily towards my goal of possessing positive attitudes at all times, but I am always prepared to learn something new and beneficial. My Leadership title is always available to an Advanced PAC Practitioner who has shown greater worthiness of the role.

So . . . we are moving rapidly on to more advanced stages of the formula for success, and I want you to thoroughly acknowledge yourself as a contender for my job, if, that is, you have embraced and begun practising the technology contained in this book as a PAC Practitioner ... but there's a way to go yet.

You should realise that affirmations can also be used for short-term gain. You can make them up for specific day-to-day activities. You can also programme yourself each night before you sleep to wake up cheerfully and optimistically at exactly 7 a.m. perhaps.

Don't try this ... *trying is always trying*. You must have *faith* and just do it! It is no good learning how to work the SM without ever utilising the knowledge. Put the alarm clock in another room, and tell yourself what time you want to wake up, and what mood you desire to wake up in. Demand results!

What do people do once they know about the SM and CM? They like themselves enough, know about positive affirmations, and take responsibility for themselves. They forgive all and sundry for anything and everything. *They learn to unravel the age-old secret of success.*

A formula was made famous by Napoleon Hill in his widely acclaimed book published in the 1930s, *Think and Grow Rich*. Hill said that the secret of great wealth would reveal itself at least once in every chapter of his book, and you would recognise the formula if you were ready for it. The other part of the equation would already be within you if you were ready for great riches.

I think we are ready to talk about *whatever you can hold in your mind* ...

STAGE THREE

Whatever you can hold in your mind

'What the mind can conceive and believe, the mind can achieve' Napoleon Hill

Guglielmo Marconi told his friends that he believed there was a way to send human voices through the air without the aid of wires. They thought he was insane and took him to be psycho-analysed. He proved himself correct, of course, by inventing wireless telegraphy.

Do you believe in telepathy?

Do you think it is possible to hold a picture in your mind, and have someone else tune in to that thought? If you do believe this simple fact, then how can it benefit you? We are learning how to use the magnificent power of the SM, and not how to defend ourselves from it.

You can't ever win by defending!

Telepathy works, and exists as a phenomenon to be utilised. How many times has someone called you, and the first thing you say with surprise is that you were just thinking about them? It often happens between my wife and me. She will say something to me and I'll tell her that I was thinking of that item not a minute prior. I have been known to answer her and she will turn around and tell me that she hadn't verbalised the question . . . it had only been an unspoken thought in her head.

Years ago, I had the ability to know the time to within a minute or so. I didn't own a watch from choice, as I felt they were uncomfortable around the wrist . . . yet I always knew the time. It became my party trick after a while, as my friends realised this unusual ability in me, and quite naturally wanted to be there for the first time I would get it wrong! Then I decided, for whatever reason, to disregard my consideration about watches being uncomfortable. I bought a new watch and lost the ability to tell the time for myself. I'm sure that attribute would return if I was to discard the watch!

It is beyond comprehension that this most magnificent creation, the human being, which uses the most sophisticated computer ever made as its operation system, would leave out a simple communication process such as telepathy from its software package. Can you imagine buying a computer that couldn't talk to a printer?

A human being, without the ability to transfer the contents of its mind, or brain, to the physical universe, is a cruel idea. Show yourself pictures of a fabulous holiday destination, and then tell yourself that you can't go there. Cruel, isn't it?

Thank goodness we have the ability to hold a picture or an idea in our minds, and then have it become a physical reality! This is a gift which needs to be used. You need to practise. You have to decide what you want, mock that picture up in your head, and give it life. Charge it with emotion and faith, love and sex, desire and yearning.

Accomplishment must be achieved in the mind before physical manifestation of that success can be achieved!

The demands that you place on your SM must be combined with the catalysts of *faith and strong emotion.*

This is how the SM works: begin with the command and the feelings . . . the SM loves the feelings . . . feelings and *faith* . . . desire . . . desire and the exhilaration you will feel through this accomplishment . . . *love* . . . the love and the sex that go with the desire . . . the yearning . . . the demand . . . the intention . . . the refusal to compromise . . . positive thought. *If honour, integrity, philanthropy and altruism form part of your desire, then this success formula triples its power* . . . if you can concentrate on giving then you will always have.

You Can Always Get What You Want with the above formula! If your formula includes giving to others . . . you will always have what you want!

Demand the physical existence of whatever it is you want. If it is money . . . see the cash and the reason for having it, look at the currency, touch those banknotes in your head just as easily as if they were on a table in front of you. Get the feelings! See what service you are willing to offer in exchange for that cash, and at the same time see the joy that this money will bring to yourself and others.

Formulate a plan

Mix emotion with desire . . . blend the ingredients harmoniously . . . then go and make it happen.

You are in charge! A person without a plan can

only drift with the tide and be the effect of other people's desires. The stronger the plan, the bigger the engine. Big engines are powerful and can negotiate fast currents. Big engines and big plans will take you where you want to go.

You have to creatively visualise your desire before it will physically appear!

You wouldn't build a house without planning it first, and referring to those plans throughout the process of building, would you? Can you imagine telling a builder to erect a house for you with four bedrooms and two reception rooms? Would a complaint be fair if you viewed the finished product for the first time and discovered that the house didn't have a garage or a bathroom? You didn't tell the builder . . . he didn't know your plans!

A movie director wouldn't consider commissioning a song for a scene in his film without briefing the songwriter, or better still showing the songwriter a rough cut of the scene. Can you imagine a heavy metal discordant bash accompanying a sweet love scene; or an Irish country jig playing merrily as a cat was run over by a car? You must order your life accurately!

Tell life what you want and it will obey!

Visualise the finished outcome of your plan, and attach yourself to the sort of contacts and friends who will be most beneficial to your achievement of expeditious and advantageous results. Your mental pictures have to be as detailed as those house plans should have been. The car you are aiming for has to have a certain colour and a particular engine. Who sells those cars? The house has to have a well-described location and a specific view. Does the girl have blue eyes or brown hair? That man in your life has ambition as well as looks . . . what kind of ambition? How can you connect with those people who can help you get where you want to be?

We did a little exercise with a cow in a field. Remember? That illustration is an important part of this programme. It has illustrated your ability to change pictures around in your head to suit your intention. You can change your plans, you can change the colour of the car you desire, you can change course mid-stream if you think that you are making a mistake.

You are in charge . . . you make the decisions!

You enlist the help of your subconscious mind by telling it what you want to happen, and then allow it to get on with the accomplishment of its task. You have a *servant*, and you need to learn how to get the most from that *service*.

We can illustrate the power of the SM with the help of a teddy bear. Sit the teddy on a chair, and then decide that the teddy will move on to the floor. Once you have made that decision, move the teddy on to the floor. You saw that action through from the decision to the final outcome using the CM. If you had not been able to use the CM, for whatever reason, the SM would have taken over and made plans for the removal of the teddy as you desired. You would have probably left the room, only to return an hour later and move the teddy without even thinking about it. You might have said to one of your children that the teddy should be in a bedroom and would they move it. The reply might be reasonable. The child might say that it isn't doing any harm and you don't usually complain . . . it is not your usual seat anyway. You see, you have put the SM into action and it will serve you well . . . if you programme it well. I often think of it like a tapeworm when it isn't programmed properly, because it has the capacity to be stupid enough to kill you, yet it is just obeying commands.

Whatever you can hold in your mind you can have, so let's get the picture just right. Drawing it on paper can help. Writing out your goals for constant referral is essential. Formulating a plan on paper and continually redrafting it until it is perfect is highly desirable.

Use your imagination

We have two types of imagination, and it is our use of these that sets us apart from the competition. *Secondary Imagination* is the ability to get ideas from what you can see . . . from things and concepts that have already been created. It is likely that this Secondary Imagination is working for you, and you are making demands on it, every day of your life.

Premier Imagination is that which is used to pluck an idea from 'thin air'. Premier Imagination is your link to the ether waves. The sum total of every thought ever contemplated is available to you in the ether waves. The intelligence of others is available to you in the ether waves. It is possible to create something from nothing and have a totally original idea. It is also possible to apparently create something from nothing by tuning in to the ether waves. Telepathy between minds is possible through this medium.

Premier Imagination is the most exciting faculty available to you. It will provide you with hunches, plans, ideas, creations, success . . . *misery, total failure, dejection and insolvency.* For it is your *Premier Imagination* which obeys your every whim and caprice. It is this PI that lies within your SM, awaiting instruction. It needs to be used, and you need to put it to work for you right now. Keep it busy! Don't be shy. Have faith and use your *Premier Imagination* to guide you on your route to success.

Don't forget that you have to tell it what to do. PI will guide you to hell if that is the direction you have suggested. If you tell it that '*life is hard*' . . . 'it's an uphill struggle' . . . 'I can't do this, I can't do that', or anything at all negative, it will turn them into self-fulfilling prophecies.

Take the time right now to look once again over my positive affirmations in Stage Two, and you may find that you now have a greater understanding of why they are so useful.

You have to keep injecting the SM with positive commands for the PI to flourish and assist your passage to success. The PI is waiting for instruction . . . don't allow it to waste time foolishly on some casual negative thought or doubt that you may have allowed to exist in your head for however short a time period.

Thoughts are self-fulfilling prophecies! Never ever drop your guard!

Let your positive mental commands be a dominant force in your life, for the PI will go to work on making those thoughts a reality. Check your course and trim your sails. Are you heading in the right direction? Do you have the correct charts? If you changed some points of your plan a little, would that speed up the accomplishment of your goal? Have you thoroughly acknowledged your *Premier Imagination*, or are you *in doubt?*

You can have faith . . . or you can be faithless

Your success begins with faith in your ability to achieve it. You must have faith in every constituent part of your route to success: faith that forgiveness has set you on your way; faith that by filling your head so full of positivity there is no alternative but to succeed; faith in your ability to like yourself and others; faith in the PAC; faith in *Premier Imagination*; faith in the SM; faith in your chosen route; and faith in your actions.

There is no room for cynicism, pessimism, mistrust, suspicion, misgivings, doubt and apprehension. They are all close relatives of abject failure. They tend to encourage bouts of depression and gloom. There is no space in a successful life for duplicity, as this involves a fear and suspicion of others . . . duplicity is not simple and straightforward, but success is. I am leading you on course for true success. I am not talking about transient success, I am dealing in true success.

Whenever I talk to people about goals I always encourage them to plan their lives with as much naivety as possible, *to begin with*.

Do not qualify your goals!

When you are first discovering yourself and exploring your inner senses for direction, just let goals flow from you without embarrassment or guilt. Ask yourself the right questions. This is a powerful piece of data. Good questioning of yourself will stimulate the right answers.

If you could have anything in the world, what would it be?

If you had millions of pounds, what would you do with it?

If you could have any one good quality that you have observed in others, what is that quality?

If you could choose your job, what would you do for a living?

If you had one wish . . . ?

On the second of January, 1993, I was at a new-year-plus-one party and I bumped into an old friend of mine. I complained to him that I was just about to start another musical venture, and that the whole business seemed to me an uphill struggle. *How could a venture achieve success with that kind of negative visualisation?*

I told him that my previous product had not sold well, and how hard it was to contemplate something new so soon after failure. We had both studied the subject of goals for some time in the past, but my interest had sadly declined as I became more and more active in the music business. His interest had increased, however, as the technology was directly related to the substance of his business.

He asked me what I would like as an epitaph. Quick as a flash I replied, '*Phil Murray wrote good songs.*' His reply was that I had already accomplished that. *That was the trigger for me. He pushed the right button.*

I had so many realisations in one instant that my life was literally transformed there and then. I looked at my plans for the previous four products that I had released on the marketplace. There was no strategy whatsoever for the sale of the products. My interest had been only to write and record!

I was elated to know why my business had struggled, and we began to succeed from that moment onwards! I quickly looked back at what had happened. All the plans that I had made for the products had succeeded, but I had ultimately failed. I'd dreamed up the ventures, started my own recording and publishing companies, enlisted the help of excellent musicians, written the songs, had the covers designed and produced, then the compact discs and cassettes manufactured. I signed my company to a distribution deal and released the recordings . . . the reviews were excellent and I was proud of the products, as I still am.

The products failed in the marketplace at that time because my plan had not extended to sales. *I had not conceived the magic thoughts on the subject of selling.*

In fact, it was worse than that, because my outlook had actually taken the form of not being interested in the financial aspect of my work. That was always to be someone else's job . . . *but I didn't give anyone else the job!*

I was able to see exactly where I had veered off the track leading to success in a split second, as I remembered just what my goal had been for these products . . . *'Phil Murray songs will always get released because they are excellent songs'* . . . and sure enough they are. There had, however, been no plans for records to sell in massive quantities! I had worked on a plan that had been inconclusive. I had not visualised the final outcome as sales. I had swallowed the clichés about artistes and money, and did not want my art tainted with finance.

I do now! Taint me! Taint me!

What good is a great song if no one hears it? Great songs do not pay your way through life unless they sell. Do you see? The viewpoint must be positive and detailed at every stage, in all ways, shapes and forms!

I recently offered the exact same *epitaph* question to a friend of mine, who was having trouble deciding what to do with the rest of her life. She didn't like the question so I changed it a little to, *'after you die, how would you like to be remembered?'* She replied that she would feel pompous expecting anyone to remember her for anything.

She, of course, will have to take care to do nothing of any note at any point in her life, in the hope that her expectation is realised. The SM and PI will sure have an easy time of that aspiration!

Actually, it was a modest viewpoint that she held as being unpretentious, but really there is nothing wrong in sharing a little of your hopes and dreams with a friend or colleague, just so long as you talk about aiming for the top, your goals and aspirations . . . *to the right people!* Beware of small-mindedness and bigotry. Guard against people who tell you that your plans are too ambitious, or that you are, *'too big for your boots'*. If someone criticises you, examine their track record. Are they being helpful or envious? Do they talk in positives or negatives? Are they looking forward to the rest of their life, or do they view it as an uphill struggle with no guarantee of success?

You will attract like-minded people through telepathy. Other people tune in to the ether waves too. Premier Imagination will home in on other people's thoughts if those deliberations are attractive. Make sure that you are holding the right intentions in your head, to ensure that you don't attract the wrong events or people into your life.

Negative thoughts are a punishment you cannot afford!

Think of your head as a garden. Grow beautiful flowers, and frequently weed it! It isn't good enough to just plant the seed. Think about this gardening point of view for a moment. If you simply left the seed on top of the soil, it would probably get strangled by weeds . . . just like an idea. You plant the seed according to the instructions, and then you water it regularly. You prune as needed. You feed the young plant. You check for bugs. If you have been successful, you will be able to look at the wonderful flowers in the summer or harvest the fruit in the autumn.

Conceiving an idea is the beginning . . . making a decision is apparent . . . having intent is a bonus . . . formulating the plan is essential . . .

Advanced PAC Practitioners always get into action

They never let an idea slip by without acting on it. They trust their *Premier Imagination*. They know that this principle of success can only work with action.

A company may manufacture the finest sailing boat the world has ever seen, but the Chairman of that company must know that the product has to be sold, if the initial idea is to be ultimately successful. Advanced PAC Practitioners know that action must continue all the way down the line to the logical conclusion of the initial idea.

Postulate sales . . . *if selling is part of your plan!*

I shudder to think how many truly beautiful songs exist in bedrooms around the world, in demo form, unavailable for anyone else's enjoyment . . . for the ears of their creator only! The dream must have been within the songwriter to begin with. The creator must have had a positive attitude at the onset of the process. Writing a song takes more positivity than negativity; negativity can creep in through the back door and stop a project in its tracks! It's your choice . . . PA or NA? The latter is a swear word in my environment. I have taught my children to challenge me any time they feel that I am criticising them destructively. And they do! Occasionally, of course, it has been known for them to throw down the challenge to hide the fact that they have just done something they felt they should not have done. But as a rule it works. When I hear the words, '*Dad, is that destructive criticism?*' I always check myself. If it is, I apologise.

You see, I think that there are few things on earth worse than continually challenging a child's viewpoint, or telling that child that he or she is always wrong, or convincing children they are stupid, horrible, small or unwanted, laughing at their mispronunciations, or exclaiming surprise that they didn't know something that has not even found its way into the Encyclopedia Britannica yet!

These attitudes perform no service for anyone . . . they bring harm into the world and plant seeds of failure in an innocent child. The SM is working overtime in young people, and serving them well! Every time that it is called stupid, it goes on to prove that self-fulfilling prophecy correct.

Ban NA and destructive criticism from your lives!

This will aid every aspect of your existence, and certainly halt the progress of any negative thoughts that had slipped through your net of surveillance. Thoughts such as . . . *'this is just too hard'* . . . *'even he couldn't do it'* . . . *'maybe next time'* . . . *'it's just not my day'* . . . *'I wasn't cut out for it anyway'*, are all examples of beliefs that should diminish in the light of a positive attitude.

Just as the idea has to be right, its execution must also be thorough. With the exclusion of NA, as you proceed on your path to success, the SM and PI will present you with answers, hunches, long shots and sure-fire certainties . . . but you must not sit back in complacency when there is so much work still to be completed.

It's time to assemble your supergroup

There is no such thing as a successful one-man band. Everyone needs someone at some time. Even if the one-man band plays his own songs, he still needs an audience. If his instruments are self-made, the materials come from elsewhere. His influences must have come from a place other than his own personal universe . . . he still needs other people in order to exist.

We all need other people . . . that is a joy of life

I have been in the entertainment industry throughout my career. During a particularly successful period for me whilst working in the music business, I returned to the north east and was reunited with an old school pal. He was a guitar player in a working band, and he invited me to the gig that night. I sang a few numbers with them from the old days, when we used to play together in the same group, and then my friend handed me a demo tape and asked me to try and get them a recording deal. I played the tape to my manager on my return home, and he got them a contract almost immediately, with a record company that I had been signed to previously.

Their first record was a hit!

Do you know how statistically hard it is to get a hit? In some countries it was number one in the pop charts! Does anyone know the exact recipe for a hit song in an ever-changing marketplace? I know this much . . . *it has little or nothing to do with the song*.

When the record entered the charts, word went round that the drummer wasn't talented enough for the job. I said that his drumming had got them a hit. *'Anyone can drum,'* was the answer. *'And get a hit?'* I replied. The drummer was replaced.

The song was at number five in the British charts when the first dark mutterings and rumours were voiced about the sax player. *'He only plays sax,'* I could hear. '*Have you seen him on stage*?' I replied. '*Sax playing is just an overdub, we can get someone in just for the records*,' was the answer. '*But he's good fun and adds sparkle*,' I replied. The band parted company with the sax player.

The studio was booked for the next recording. Someone said that the bass player couldn't play a particular style of bass. '*But the band don't use that bass style*,' I replied. '*Yes, but Rod Stewart's bass player is available for the session*,' was the excuse. '*But the bass player has been with the band forever*,' I replied, '*and he's good*.' The bassist said his farewells with as much dignity as he could muster, and the keyboard player followed him under similar circumstances.

Now the two songwriters remained . . . my pal the guitarist, and the singer. The two follow-up record releases had floundered. '*It's only the voice that people hear*,' was the phrase of that moment. '*But the guitarist is one of the best I've ever heard and he's my friend*,' I replied. '*The singer can write with anyone, and we can get him a solo deal in the States*,' was the final excuse.

Before the singer actually went solo, he offered my friend a smaller percentage on their writing partnership . . . he saw his role as the singer and senior member. Thankfully my friend walked away from that unhealthy situation, and sadly we all said goodbye to a fine band.

It was the group members, with their individual attitudes and attributes, that made the band successful; the magic merging of the single entities into a group, and not just selfish performances brought together without fusion. The merged minds of the human beings caused the positive vibrations. *Success waiting to happen* occurs when goals from various constituent parts of an organisation are aligned. Members of a group tune into the same wavelength and walk the path together. They contribute to the master plan in unique ways. A half-decent drummer may be the heart and soul of the band. There may be better drummers . . . but does a drummer just drum?

Goals must be tuned and honed, careful plans made, then action must occur

How many times have the Beatles been discussed as an after-dinner topic? *'What a lucky break for Ringo'* . . . *'That George was just along for the ride'* . . . *'John writes better on his own'* . . . *'It was Paul's looks'* . . . *'George Martin showed them the chords, you know.'* I always thought that it was the five of them together!

I always saw that successfully creative team as having five members. The magic occurred between them. $1 + 1 + 1 + 1 + 1 = 25$. The phenomenon was the group. You might say that you liked John the best . . . but that didn't make him the main reason for their phenomenal success and group talent.

I worked with a famous producer for a while. I learnt many things from him, particularly the way he viewed his role. He saw himself as a catalyst. He called himself the communication point for the group, and asked that all ideas be channelled through him.

Our drummer thought that this person was inferior as a producer, that he was incapable of conveying our music to tape, and told him so. Unfortunately, this particular producer also owned the record company to which we were contracted. The producer told the drummer that he quit and the job was his. The drummer later apologised when no more studio time was forthcoming from the record company. The point of the anecdote is . . . the producer's role and interpretation of the production task was not acknowledged, and of course we needed him because he was *part of the formula*. It wasn't the same without him!

Form your own Supergroup

You will need a Nuclear Supergroup and an Extended Supergroup. The Nuclear Supergroup will comprise the people necessary for the smooth and expansive running of your life. You will head this group, regardless of your leadership capabilities. Next will be your spouse and children. Then the remainder of your family will fit around your plans, dependent upon practicalities. Also, there are your employees, workmates, bosses or colleagues to include.

Now we will work on the Extended Supergroup. Can you see that when two people get together with a common purpose, a third force is created? Not only do you have your own viewpoint and that of your colleague, but you also have the third force which is the result of the combination of the two viewpoints. $1 + 1 = 3$.

Now is the time to assemble the team who will make up your Supergroup. Naturally, a team of Advanced PAC Practitioners is highly desirable, but we must always remember that in this case the goal is senior to the method, and it could be that the most depressing misanthropist in existence just happens to be the contact with the formula for the accomplishment of the next stage of your goal. I certainly wouldn't allow permanent membership to such a fellow, but I would develop a working relationship with him and thus afford him a glimpse of a lower harmonic of my Supergroup.

The nucleus of my Extended Supergroup comprises Advanced PAC Practitioners only; people holding similar philanthropic, spiritual and altruistic beliefs. My wife is in my Extended Supergroup in addition to the Nuclear Supergroup. Such a decision is personal and is entirely dependent on individual circumstances. Different marriages and relationships work in a variety of ways. I have a friend whose business is totally unrelated to mine, but our common ground is PAC membership. He is part of my Extended Supergroup, which presently has a membership of eight. I aim for ten as full membership.

Unless you are very fortunate indeed, you will find that membership is not necessarily permanent, although in an ideal world it would be. The purpose of the Extended Supergroup is *interdependent assistance*. The group should meet regularly if this is possible . . . I do, however, know of groups that are unable to do this, yet agree that a loose telepathic bond between them serves a similar purpose. Agreement for success is the important sentiment. You may seek solutions to your problems from your Supergroup. You should expect contacts to be forthcoming. If you have a wealthy member, then perhaps you can arrange for this associate to finance your loan requirements, rather than take them outside your group.

The Extended Supergroup is an interdependent entity

Don't forget your obligation for giving to this group. It will be as strong as it has *giving members*, but its principle lies within the equation $1 + 1 = 3$. You will have access to brains that are not in your head, and experience that is not from your past. Different combinations of members will provide assorted solutions to a variety of questions. Advanced PAC Practitioners, by their very definition, always succeed, and a group of pooled resources from such an assembly will have awesome power. Use this data as soon as possible and get your Supergroup into action. Don't dump rubbish on this association of colleagues. Accomplish what you can alone . . . then take the trickier questions to your Supergroup. Respect a member's privacy. Build firmly on mutual understanding and common ground.

Jot down the names of twenty people that you would consider for membership. Next to each name, write the reason why you would like them in your group. Whittle the candidates down to a manageable ten. Casually begin to discuss your ideas for such a venture with each candidate. You could strike lucky and have someone turn around to you right away and say what a good idea you have just presented them with, or you may have to start again from scratch. Begin now. If you feel that this idea has merit . . . have *faith* and get into action!

This is one more step on your road to personal success. I advise you at this point in the book to consider being the insurer of your own happy future, by guaranteeing your success right now. Find like-minded people who are willing to interpledge support. Go on . . . make that simple decision to excel in whatever enterprise you may be engaged in. Be excited. Assemble your Supergroup, and banish NA from it, along with destructive criticism and low expectations. *Get the picture of your goal just how you want it, and hold that idea and plan in your mind until it becomes a physical reality.*

Don't ever be afraid to own money, because *money brings joy to the enlightened* . . .

STAGE FOUR

Money brings joy to the enlightened

'Riches begin in the mind' Phil Murray

You cannot escape the fact that you need money in this world. You may also have noticed that most of us are *too busy earning a living to make money*. We have designed the game in such a way that finance is absolutely essential for most aspects of life. We throw ourselves awkward curves by making certain aspects of money politically incorrect. In Britain, if one has more money than another we are told not to flaunt it . . . *just hope that it is noticed!*

We have shrouded money in a cloak of mystery and fabricated lies about it. Perhaps you have heard a few of these lies somewhere before . . . *'you cannot be artistic and into money as well'* and the biggest misquote of them all . . . *'money is the root of all evil.'* Another old saying holds perhaps more truth than we care to admit, but nevertheless is not always the case . . . *'The best things in life are free.'* Other sayings include . . . *'Money isn't everything'* (an excuse for not having any!) . . . *'Spiritual people don't need money'* . . . *'Friendships and money just don't mix.'*

Do you want to know what I say? *Give me the cash!*

Give me the cash in any currency that buys what I want. Hand me the money! Dish the dosh! Put the notes on the table. Let's talk in financial terms. Dollars, pounds, deutschmarks and yen! I can see cases full of the stuff. I make my £50 notes into a wedge and carry them on my hip. *I've got loads of money. It's a rich man's world and I'm a rich man!*

Get the picture? Let's put the myth to rest that there is anything vulgar about money.

Money is simply an exchange

Before money, people traded possessions directly. All we have done in this day and age is place money in the middle of transactions that involve the exchange of goods between people. You sell something and take money for it, until you know what you want to spend that money on, and then you pass the money to the owner of whatever you want to buy. Money itself is worthless. It is the agreements we have made about money that are valuable.

Money is not powerful, it is helpless. It needs you to inject it with purpose

Money requires assistance in deciding what to do with itself. You can decide to use world considerations about money to make yourself look powerful, but that is just a quick fix of vanity. We are seeking long-term personal success for every aspect of our lives.

Let's make one thing quite clear . . . there is so much money in the world it's incredible, an absolute abundance! There are zillions of types and units of currency out there, and we call them by all sorts of names. There are *dollars and pounds, marks and lire, schillings and punts, yen and roubles, drachmas and shekels* . . . all there for your use.

All you have to do is provide a service that is needed or wanted, and someone will give you money in direct proportion to the grade of service you supply. If you want lots of money, then you must ensure that you supply a service that people are willing to pay dearly for.

It is no good postulating a vast fortune for yourself, then taking a job as a waiter until it shows up. You can visualise yourself as the best waiter who ever served a meal to a table, but history has shown that this job does not yield as great a financial reward as other professions such as accountancy or perhaps entertainment. *Getting into full action mode means action in the right direction.*

So, we are getting money in perspective. We are agreed on the fact that you need money in order to live in this world, and we know about visualising.

Visualise yourself with lots of money! Riches begin in the mind!

Decide exactly how much money you want, and picture yourself already in possession of that money. Have *faith* in your visualisation. Decide on the currency and give yourself a realistic time limit. Be firm. *Life will give you exactly what you demand of it.* Learn from my mistakes. I produced and manufactured for four years without a good financial return as one of my goals.

Money is mainly a by-product of a goal. It would be sensible to set yourself a goal and then have the money come in as a result of achieving that goal. For instance, you could decide that you wanted to invent a shirt that does not need to be washed. That is your goal. You can bet your life, or your shirt, that when you achieve that goal, if you have marketed the product properly, you will end up a wealthy person. If you feel that cash is not a good thing for you to have, then you will probably sell the idea to someone else who is ready to enjoy the money that will come from it.

A good example of this is the fact that the Coca Cola recipe was sold for a few hundred dollars. You see, it wasn't sufficient to dream up the recipe. An ingredient was missing to make Coca Cola the financial success that it undoubtedly is. The person who bought the recipe had that missing ingredient. He visualised the next step of the Coca Cola phenomenon . . . and put it into practice!

If, however, you find yourself without any goals whatsoever except a burning desire for cash, then there is no reason at all why you shouldn't copy someone else's success.

What earns money for one, can earn money for another!

Find an idea or a person with a proven record of success. You can be certain that any successful venture has had its fair share of trials and tribulations . . . there is no reason at all why mistakes should have to be made twice. You have already learned from my expensive lesson that if you want money you should always make it a part of your visualisation process. So if you want to own a launderette, and you site it on an estate where everyone owns their own washing machine, and John, your mate from the pub, had already tried one there and gone bust, you must not be surprised if you struggle.

What I am urging you to do is copy success

You have seen this happen in the music business. The Beatles came along and spawned a thousand imitators. A few of the groups that copied them were absolutely excellent in their own right. Some used the Beatles as inspiration only, while others copied the chord progressions and the harmonies. A number of pop group managers copied the success formula of the Beatles' manager.

You can see this taking place in manufacturing. The Sony Walkman generated an awful lot of imitations, while car styles are duplicated, then customised just enough to make them almost individual. Firms allow their rivals to test a product in the marketplace before committing themselves and their cash to a similar commodity. *There are trendsetters, and trend followers. Both systems can make you vast sums of money!*

If you want lots of cash, find someone who is already making lots of cash, and in the absence of any other goal of your own, copy them.

If you want to hold on to your money, it seems to be a good idea to always keep 10% for yourself. Whatever inflow of cash comes your way, just take 10% straight off the top, and keep it in the bank, building society or some other safe place. *Make your money reproduce itself.* Let someone give you more money for the privilege of looking after your cash. *On no account must you ever spend this money!* This is your estate and security.

You will even find that some people want to give you more money just because you own money. Just let this money gather momentum of its own accord and surround you with a feeling of security.

Money gives you the luxury of being able to say no, and hold out for better deals. Without money, you run the risk of taking the first offer that comes along out of desperation.

I doubt there is a self-made millionaire in existence who has not, and does not borrow money.

Now I must be careful in the way that I transmit this theory to you . . . my intention is not to give the impression that you can just borrow to make yourself rich. *I am talking about the use of other people's money as the financial energy necessary for the execution of a worthy goal.* I don't support borrowing for the sake of it. The goal is the reason for the loan. I do think it is important to emphasise the rules of the game at this stage.

Borrowing is the capitalist way

The industry of Great Britain, and indeed the rest of the developed world, exists because its founders were able to borrow. There is always money available for a good practical idea. If you have your goal well visualised, written out and planned in fine detail, and you get into full action mode, you will get all of the money you need . . . *if the person you are dealing with can see the validity of your plan.* If not, then you need to *find the financier who has been seeking such a plan.*

The Bible states that *'love of money is the root of all evil'* . . . greeding, lusting and worshipping the stuff is my interpretation of that line. George Bernard Shaw said that *'lack of money is the root of all evil.'* I believe that money is the root cause of many problems in the world, but we must remember the pleasure its unselfish presence can also bring. Let us be clear on the fact that money itself is nothing at all, only what it seems to the individual viewpoint. It isn't a building or an industry, it cannot fly or drive you anywhere. It is merely significance. Focus on the good things that can be accomplished with well-ordered finances . . . the building of schools and hospitals, the furtherance of brilliant ideas, and of course pleasure!

You will definitely need money, and an Advanced PAC Practitioner has no problems getting it, increasing its value, and holding on to it as long as is necessary. So if you need some cash for the financing of your newly conceived goal, as long as your plans are sound and your purpose honourable, borrow at the lowest rate possible, from the highest-profile institution of good repute, and preferably on personal recommendation from more than one source.

Premier imagination will help you get the money you need to get started

You have to remember that there are people out there whose sole purpose of employment is to invest a client's money in a potentially winning scheme. There are fund managers whose statistics are based on their ability to get rid of money that is lying around not earning its keep, into ventures that have a steady chance of flourishing. You have to link up with this energy. There is nothing more heartening to a well-balanced fund manager with excess cash, than to be presented enthusiastically with a sound idea, and a request for financial assistance with which to fulfil the potential of that concept.

Don't expect your bank manager to understand anything other than concrete ideas . . . they rarely deal in the abstract, as I have discovered many times to my misfortune. They like to view statistics on pieces of paper. If you have an idea for a product, they usually like to see orders for it . . . to view with their eyes in preference to the use of intuition. Do not let their style inhibit you . . . it need not impinge on your creativity, in fact they do not really need to know anything that is conceptually within you. If you are going to the financial institutions for money, show them that you can play the game their way.

Don't fight the financial system . . . use it

Be wise in your borrowing. Look for the very best terms, and don't ever be afraid to question even the highest-profile outfit on the high street, to see if you can improve on those terms. I have saved so much money during my life, just through the wise use of words. My wife Allison is also well versed in the art of presenting her case for financial gain. As long as everyone wins, I actually feel I am performing a service to the person with whom I am haggling.

In the 1970s, Allison and I went shopping for a jacket each in London. We had a budget of £100 each. I quickly found one that suited me fine and I purchased it within the budget. In the shop next door there was a jacket that my wife fell in love with. It was £120. We looked at each other knowingly, and entered the shop. I told the owner that our budget was £100 but the jacket that we liked in his window was £120, and would he mind reducing it to £100? He asked if we would mind increasing our budget to £120 and laughed at us. We bandied words for a while, but I knew the profit margin on this jacket would be in the region of 100%, *so I felt good about giving him the profit that he would still be getting if he sold us the jacket for £100.*

He sold it to us for £100, and it was a fair deal

for all involved. A win for him and a win for us!

You have to be able to ride the waves when you try for good prices. I saw a studio quality cassette recorder that had been reduced from £800 down to £400. I asked the assistant why this was so, and he told me that it had been in the showroom for two years, and they had used it as a demonstration model to sell from stock. This was now the last one, and they were discontinuing that particular version.

I knew they were selling it at cost price, but I also knew that they had already made huge profits on it during the two years that it had served them well. I asked for the manager, and offered him £200, with an accompanying explanation. He laughed at me. I rode the wave. He wasn't used to selling beneath what an item had cost him, and I was introducing him to the idea that he had actually already made his money on the product. I felt that I was offering a fair deal that offered each party a win. He sold it to me for £200.

Whenever I went into the shop after that, he expected to give me a good deal. We did lots of business together.

You see, my goal is not to *get one over on someone, or screw them into the ground* . . . and I expect that attitude to reflect back on to me. My goal is to win, and I believe that it is always possible for the other person to win at the same time. *I call this my 'win for all' ingredient.*

We had a mortgage with a building society, who we discovered were charging us 1% above the normal interest rate for our home loan because that particular house had the right to semi-commercial use. It was a year before I realised that this was occurring. I telephoned the company and spoke to the manager. I told him that I didn't want to pay the extra, and what's more, *I wanted the overpayment refunded.* He laughed, but I rode the wave. We talked some more, and he agreed to the reduction back down to domestic rate . . . *and to the refund!* He didn't want to lose my custom, saw that I had a good case, and knew I could get home finance elsewhere . . . I stayed with them for many years.

It is wise to adopt good selling techniques when buying

A conversational approach works well . . . and communicating on the same wavelength as the person you are dealing with is essential. Visualisation of the desired final result as already accomplished is necessary, and slight mimicry is also a proven part of the formula.

Do not alienate yourself from someone by being too different. Find out what that person is aspiring towards . . . and be the personification of his desire. If he likes football, talk football. If you see that he is keen on something, and you don't have a clue about any aspect of that something, tell him you had always wanted to know more about it and let him explain. If you have a general interest in life with a positive attitude, it will always be true that you do want to know about something of which you are presently ignorant.

Physical mimicry works, but can sometimes be too obvious. I prefer to just *be myself*, but if you must use this trick then you have to be subtle about it. If you talk like Prince Charles and you are trying to sell to Paul Gascoigne, it may help if you tone the upper-class accent down a little . . . unless your customer is aspiring towards your style of speech of course. If he scratches his nose, you have to be able to scratch yours without really thinking about it. These thoughts in the CM are telepathic, however, and depending on the awareness of the person you are with, he could tune in and feel that you are being facetious, to put it politely.

This is an honourable way of doing business, just as it would be if you learnt German to engage in business with a customer who spoke German. It is a method of communication.

A simple warning will suffice for any unscrupulous individuals who find themselves in possession of this book, and the powerful data contained herein. Firstly, I doubt if it is possible for you to absorb the finer points without an accompanying honourable purpose. Secondly, and more importantly, don't try and do anything other than good with the technology contained in this book. *It is all based on a simple karmic fact of life. . . what you give you get!* Whatever your action or transmission, like phenomena will return your way, just like a boomerang . . .

This data, used for a dishonourable purpose, will destroy you!

You must have a good ethical code of conduct, and it must always take precedence over any scheme you may be contemplating that has a question mark attached to it. Refer to your inner values and trust them. Don't ever compromise with what you feel is correct.

Your ethical code of good and bad, right and wrong, needs to be regularly reviewed. Your inner values are more deeply rooted and frequently of greater value. It is a well-known fact that people only engage in acts that they think are right. Criminals don't rob, deceive and kill because they think it's wrong. They think that it is right for them. Surveys have shown that when people first come into contact with crime, they feel an abhorrence. After they have taken part in criminal activity, they feel uncomfortable . . . when they have been around crime and criminals for a length of time, it feels right. You need to live and make your money honestly.

Your SM needs to be around powerful, ethically correct stimuli

Another good financial idea is to give some of your cash away to make room for a new influx. Keep money flowing. Give to charity. When everyone else donates a pound, you should make it your business to give three! Find an organisation you enjoy giving to . . . then give!

Most people are *too busy earning a living to make money!* Do remember this aphorism if you find that your everyday lifestyle of habits and traditions gets in the way of true progress along your chosen path. Stay fresh and lively, with eyes open wide for sight of honest opportunity.

It's easier being spiritual with a pound in your pocket than it is on an empty stomach!

Once money begins to flow in your direction, remember that you are only playing a game in the physical world. Do not let that game dominant your beingness just because you are winning. This is the time to invest in the world that you really belong to. Let your money give you the time to study and discover more about the real you.

Read what the great prophets have had to say through the ages. There are some terrific ideas out there for the pondering. The idea of karma . . . *what you give you get . . . doing to others only those things that you would not mind others doing to yourself . . . you sow what you reap . . . you are what you think you are.*

The greater the quantity of good inspirational material you read, the more able you will be to absorb new ideas and philosophies . . . and the easier your path to profit will be. When you find an author you like, look out for his or her recommendations. Does the book have a bibliography? If so, don't just read it . . . go and get the books it recommends and continue with your progress.

Do you need specific books for your business? Do you have the manuals necessary for the smooth operation of your machinery? Do you feel good about giving specific books as presents to employees . . . or employers?

Do you waste time watching TV? Do you realise the TV is constantly on in the background? Do you go down to the pub when you should be hard at work travelling your route to great wealth? You have to contribute the necessary quality hours of labour in order to succeed. Part of this work is reading and researching . . . don't ever feel guilty about the amount of time you spend honestly studying for the furtherance of your purpose in life.

You can search deeply or superficially. The more spiritual you are in your outlook, the fuller your physical life will be. Play the body game to its highest level of enjoyment, but always remember that when the game of life is up, you as a spiritual entity will still exist . . . answerable to yourself and responsible for your own karma. This data is not a threat. Use it as knowledge to further enhance your present life and enjoy yourself even more. New personal awareness should never equal self-intimidation, and any fear that arrives with new abilities into your mental capacity, should be channelled positively into a karmic self-checking system.

You are invited to the party. A few rules and guidelines will help you achieve fulfilment. Whilst looking at the picture that I am painting, please remember that there is nothing wrong with borrowing cash, or owning cash . . . just put it to good use!

You have money, you are operating on a physical and a spiritual plane, you are a kind and forgiving person, you like yourself and others, you have goals, dreams and honourable aspirations. Let me ask you this, *who is in charge now . . . you or your mind*?

STAGE FIVE

Who is in charge now ... you or your mind?

'You do not need to be an electronic engineer, or a physicist, to operate your own servo-mechanism, any more than you have to be able to engineer an automobile in order to drive one, or become an electrical engineer in order to turn on the light in your room' Maxwell Maltz

By now, you should be feeling the power that is yours to possess forever. There should be fullness of purpose intrinsically within everything that you do and think ... *and you should know who is in charge.* If there are any unfulfilling habits remaining within your modus operandi that are not advantageous, then it may be an idea to turn your attention to changing them for the better. If you have not modified old, unworkable considerations as you have been reading this manual, then now is a good time to effect useful change.

You may have some physical problems that are holding you back and stunting your progress. You must do your best to get your body into shape. If this involves effort then take it easy and approach the challenge intelligently.

Get yourself into fully fit mode

If you are planning to enjoy success fully, it is wise to have your body in a healthy state. I'm not talking about anything unattainable here. I'm not suggesting that a bank clerk needs to be as fit as an athlete, or a fireman needs the strength of Superman.

You need to be fit enough for the lifestyle you are contemplating

If you would like to give up smoking, for instance, then I suggest that you give smoking an undesirable image. Tell yourself that you have a healthy body, and get a picture in your head of that undesirable image every time you want to smoke. If there is a type of behaviour that you do not enjoy in other people, associate that behaviour with smoking. Smell an ashtray. Visit a patient who has just had a lung removed. Confront the phlegm that patient is coughing up. Check your teeth for nicotine stains.

All the time you are focusing on the negative, you are doing it from a positive point of view. If your sense of smell has suffered, aspire towards its return to full strength. Try smelling your favourite flower. If you cannot sense the scent, dub it in. Tell your mind that you can smell it. Remember the aroma from the last time you could smell that type of flower.

If you have physical withdrawal symptoms, then you must stamp your authority on the situation even more heavily. Other people have given up, so why shouldn't you? They got through the pain, so you can too. Just give up and accept nothing less than being a non-smoker. Take pleasure in sitting at the *no smoking* table at work, or in the *no smoking* compartment of a train. Make the pleasure immense when you reply, *'non-smoking'*, to the girl at the airline check-in desk.

You have to make it seem better for you to not smoke, than it is for you to indulge in the habit. It is the same with whatever you do. Make what you want to do seem attractive, and what you don't want, utterly contemptible. See the pleasure in your success, and if you want to contemplate failure at all, make it a dismally miserable experience that passes quickly.

You know, smoking is a dilemma of our time whether we are able to confront the problem or not. In a well-balanced Advanced PAC Practitioner, I have to say that there is no excuse whatsoever for smoking. You have the technology at your disposal to rid yourself of the damaging habit. I have been through it . . . I know what I am talking about!

When I began to smoke at school many years ago, I had to compel myself to like it, but once I had obliged the curiosity within by smoking a few cigarettes, *they forced me to continue*! My journey to dominance over the habit began from an observation of my eighty-year-old grandmother, who came to stay with us for a holiday back in 1981. She had smoked for seventy years. One evening, as we were settling into the lounge for a chat, she lit up a cigarette, took a puff from it, and threw it into the coal fire. *'That was my last,'* she exclaimed.

All it took for her to accomplish this simple task was a decision and a positive purpose. She had no withdrawal symptoms because *she didn't expect any*.

Six months later my mother gave up the habit after forty years. Then my parents came to stay with us for a holiday. My father, who was then sixty-eight years old, and had been smoking for almost sixty of those years, stubbed out a cigarette and said, *'No more!'*

I was embarrassed. What would I do? I was studying

the workings of the mind and improving my mental abilities at the time, and I was encouraging my family to do the same. Yet they were able to kick a nasty habit so easily, and I was still wading in with the old excuse that I had reached a mental state where I was able to do anything I wanted . . . and I wanted to smoke!

I wasn't the only one. It was the single most used excuse amongst my peers at the time. We were all travelling the path to mental and spiritual freedom, and so many of us used this same justification. I did stop, however, and the withdrawal symptoms were atrocious! My willpower was fierce and I won the confrontation, even though I put on two stones in weight . . . *just as I had expected!*

Affirmations can assist you: *I enjoy being a non-smoker. I enjoy being a non-smoker. I enjoy being a non-smoker. I have a healthy body!*

There is nothing that smoking can provide you with that is not available non-toxically elsewhere. I have heard most of the justifications for continuing with the habit – the relaxation excuse . . . rubbish; the image excuse . . . garbage. Anything that you can think of that is pro-smoking is wrong. Get it? So if you have not given up by now, then just do it and let us elevate the lesson into more desirable contemplations.

I have a little more empathy for the overeater, but not much. I was two stones overweight before having the good fortune to come across Harvey and Marilyn Diamond's eating regime in the book *Fit for Life*, which has now been superseded by *Fit for Life Two*. Principally, both books are about food combining and healthy eating routines. Although they are not strictly vegetarian publications, I was heavily into vegetarianism, and knew every single veggie argument off by heart, with my own special twists and turns which were guaranteed to shock and sicken. When meat-eaters saw me coming their mental sighs of helplessness were almost audible.

I was a bigot as well. I didn't greet my friends with hello . . . I'd launch immediately into a tirade about animal rights and vegetable protein. I could clear a room instantly just by being there with my veggie bigotry. The potency of my argument was augmented by my quarrelling ability. I cannot remember a single time when a friend or colleague got the better of me. I thought this was a terrific attribute . . . but they didn't. All I did was alienate my friends by holding on to a viewpoint despite them. The viewpoint took precedence over my friendship with them. I had a good cause, but no one took note because of the intolerant delivery.

I am still vegetarian, as are my daughter, Eve, my son, Luke, and my wife, Allison. We felt that our children should ease up on their principled crusade, as they had become more biased and prejudiced than ourselves regarding this topic. We took them to a burger bar and ordered the meatiest burgers that were on offer, whether they approved of the idea or not. I ate mine, and insisted that they ate theirs. They wouldn't, they just wouldn't, and they were disgusted that I had eaten mine with the knowledge they knew I had about the subject. I ate theirs as well, just to make myself right. I tried to enjoy meat for a short time after that but it was a plain fact that I did not like it!

I told them all the reasons why they should eat meat, but the case was totally inconclusive and they wouldn't budge on the issue. It wasn't until I had presented them with all the alternative viewpoints, that I felt good about them continuing as vegetarians. They gave me a rough time about that particular episode though, because I had not approached the challenge from a healthy viewpoint. Even though I continued as a vegetarian, they deried me as a meat-eater for a long time afterwards.

My purpose here is not to espouse the cause or habit of vegetarianism. It is merely to point you in the direction of alternative eating customs that you may like to explore. You could discover that the absence of meat from your diet is a positive change. You may wish to become a part-time veggie. You could consider being a *fishie*, a fish-only person . . . my recommendation is to give it a try. Get yourself a book from the library on the moral issue. Read another about the health aspect of meat-eating. At the very least, make a well-informed judgement about the subject, and whatever your decision may be, feel good about it.

The mistake I made when I became vegetarian, was in thinking that I could eat as much as I liked. I was mistaken. The worst thing you can do is overeat, whether you are a vegetarian or meat-eater.

Push that plate away when you have had enough. Get into the habit of leaving something on your plate. If you still want to eat for the taste trip, but know that your stomach is full, push that plate away and turn up your favourite music . . . loud! Introduce pleasure into the equation. Sing at the top of your voice. Turn your attention to something other than food, stomach or taste . . . see yourself in the next size down if you are too fat.

Some simple yet useful affirmations are . . . *I'm a good weight for my height. I'm a good weight for my height. I'm a good weight for my height. I'm a good weight for my height. I eat all the right things and I look just right!*

There is a clever little trick that can work for you. Take chocolate as an example. I used to really enjoy chocolate and consequently ate too much of it. I loved the taste and the texture. I hated the taste and texture of lard, however. To wean myself off chocolate, I substituted the mental sensation of lard for the ones I associated with chocolate. Eating chocolate became eating lard to all intents and purposes. Whenever I ate chocolate, I thought lard.

You can do this with anything. I call the trick . . . *mental substitution.*

It is the art of taking a desirable yet unhealthy craving, and substituting an undesirable feeling for the mental outlook you have on that fixation. Thus, chocolate becomes lard.

Drugs are the menace of our age. I am not an expert on drugs or medicine, and can tell you only of my limited but interesting experiences.

In 1976, I became a member of an almost drug-free culture. It was a prerequisite of the course for spiritual enlightenment that I had embarked on, and I had embraced the idea excitedly. I have rarely needed drugs since the day I agreed to do without them wherever possible. But let me make one thing quite clear. If I needed drugs for a sound medical reason, *and I would be the main judge of that, then I would take them.*

I am talking about cough medicine, cold remedies, headache pills, painkillers and other everyday drugs available over the counter at the pharmacy. I exclude antibiotics from this list. There are usually other methods of treating an ailment without resorting to drugs. I have read in various reports, that psychosomatic illness accounts for up to 90% of the cases that are treated by general practitioners every day. That means illness induced by the mind . . . in other words self-inflicted!

Voodoo works in a similar way. You get the person to believe that something is going to happen and well, well, well . . . it happens. The hex voiced by someone else is eventually self-imposed.

I got out of the habit of relying on medical doctors for all but the severest of problems many years ago. I must also say that I have not had any chronic problems since I convinced myself that I had a healthy body. The moment I trusted my inner judgement and allowed it to take precedence over any other expert opinion, I became my own basic doctor. *This is not a cheap shot at members of the medical profession who I know are often overworked.* Any medical doctor who has studied beyond what was necessary in order for him or her to qualify will know that there is much more to treating patients than medicine.

If a criticism is relevant here then it is of you, if you once held and still hold the opinion that drugs are a substitute for mental power.

Advanced PAC practitioners hold their own counsel and judge according to an inner feeling

I understand that drugs are a useful assistance in the business of medicine, to the same degree that I understand they are also a last resort. If I know that the dentist's drill is going to touch a live nerve during treatment, and I know that I presently have an inability to withstand the resultant pain without jumping and shrieking at the top of my voice, then I also know that it is wise for me to have a painkilling injection in my gum, *and I have one*.

If there is no nerve in the tooth that is being worked on, then I always request treatment without the painkiller in the first instance . . . if it hurts, and gets in the way of the treatment, I request the shot.

Society must end its fixation on drugs!

It is now time to relegate drugs to the second division of the cure tables. *We must steer our approach to illness in the direction of improving mental power within the patient. Every course in medicine should begin and end with a thorough education in the basic workings of the human mind.*

I don't mean psychobabble. The days of meaningless waffle and endless droves of groovy viewpoints are over. We seek success and need to be cognisant of the ingredients. Knowledge of the spirit, mind and body are necessary for this end, and it is for this reason only that I espouse these viewpoints on medicine and drugs.

Drugs for fun? What do you think? Ultimately, as a PAC member, you will shy away from anything over which you do not have full control. I don't take drugs for fun, because I'm bigger than that. *Firstly, I made the mental decision.* My business has a lot less drug involvement than the press would have you believe. Most successful actors, actresses, singers, musicians and producers, are too busy being successful to involve themselves with drugs.

I often get calls at around nine in the evening, and I mention to the caller that I was just on my way to bed. It causes amazement. Early nights do not seem to tally with the stereotypical image of entertainers.

If you have to be on a film set on a freezing Tuesday morning at the beginning of February, in the London Docklands, at 5 a.m., you can't stay up late the night before, high on LSD, and still look good on camera whilst memorising and delivering your lines. I have worked with many famous people, and they are usually as far removed from their contrived press image as it is possible to conceive.

If drugs are controlling you . . . you are not!

If you are in the public eye, then you cannot escape your civic responsibility. You are there because of the public. You have a duty to set a good and honourable example. The image of sex, drugs and rock-n-roll doesn't hold true any more . . . if it ever did in all but the odd highly publicised instance. Nor does it have to be a kiss on the cheek, Perrier and a little light music. C'mon, you know the scene and can see what I am driving at. *PAC people enjoy what is available . . . they know when to start and how to stop.* They know when harm is a potential result of an action. They don't need to ask someone else. Advanced PAC Practitioners utilise their own value system as a guidance mechanism.

Where would we be without *Lucy in the Sky with Diamonds*? It's a tricky subject to deal with. The world would be a poorer place without the imagery created by such a song. The so-called drug-written songs of the sixties were indeed sometimes beautiful, and tugged at emotions rarely experienced by listeners. The mental image effects that were the result of such music had been infrequently used in popular music up until this time. All I can say is, *thank goodness we have the impressions from this period, and thank goodness again that the sixties have passed by, leaving a decent legacy and not too much planetary damage.* We know what hallucinatory drugs are capable of inducing . . . starry illusions! The apparitions that you may be able to see when using such drugs, and the concepts that one may feel able to embrace when under the influence of them, are all available elsewhere using safer methods. We know about the feelings and emotions that have been described from such trips.

I also know that anything you can experience

with fun drugs, you can experience safely without.

I mentioned earlier about copying. That was a reference to copying principally connected with money-making schemes. Copying can also be utilised for the achievement of other aims. You can copy good examples, good behaviour, techniques and *exhilarating experiences*. There is even good reason to believe that people with mental disabilities can be encouraged to copy other more fortunate people, and have the *apparency*, in varying degrees, of normality.

It's up to you. Challenge yourself. Phil's Potent Potion; The Magical Murray Medicine; The Drug-Free Tonic. Try them all. If you are turned on by someone's story of a drug experience . . . try having that experience without the drug. If I contemplated relying on an artificial stimulant, I would feel smaller and less in control of my life. I know that I am wiser than that! *You are too!*

I know about *walking the talk*, but please . . . if we meet and you see that I am wearing leather shoes and drinking a pint of draught beer, spare me the '*alcohol is a drug and animal skin cruelty*' arguments. I've heard them all before and perhaps even composed some of them! I do what I think is right for me at the time. I am a sentient being with circumstances that change on a daily basis. I rely on my inner values and intrinsic judgement abilities rather than tight, inflexible, self-imposed rules and regulations. I advise you to explore similar techniques.

I recently worked for the BBC, with a director who was also vegetarian. He was quick to point out that he wore plastic shoes. He said that he was so tired of that *old leather shoe* argument that he had decided to go the whole way. *Fine.* My decisions are not reliant on what other people think, even though I remain sensitive to the viewpoints of others.

Be an *aware PAC Practitioner* and do what you think is right . . . don't ever allow yourself the punishment of thinking that ignorance is an excuse. '*I didn't know*' is just about the worst excuse in the world. '*Find out*' is possibly the most effective antidote.

Drugs are a no no no area. You know that, I know that, and now we have to find new ways of showing the new generations that such is the case. One method is to increase our emphasis on good fun education on the subject. That is as important, if not more so, than an academic education . . . which of course is a big help in itself, although the fostering of an intuitive awareness would perhaps be even more expeditious. We have to get the message across to the children and prepare a positive future for them. I believe that is a duty! Show them in the home, teach them in the playground, demonstrate to them on the street. The message is simply . . .

> *I don't need drugs for a real good time*
> *I don't smoke dope and I'm feeling fine*
> *I just love life and I'm high on that*
> *I get turned on with a thought . . .*

Whatever works for you, and whatever works for the new generations, is fine by me. My purpose here is to endorse a general direction – the right direction – by taking a bearing on a *drug-free culture!*

At this point it is worth examining your primary motivation, to discover if it is basically impetus towards pleasure, or stimulus away from pain. Are you running away from poverty, or towards plenty? There is nothing wrong with either drive type. It is good to know your primary motivation mechanism so that you may utilise it more knowingly. The only thing to beware of if you are an *away from* person, is losing your drive when you have escaped poverty and finding that your motivation has sagged when you reach safety. There is no reason why you cannot have incentives from both areas, and if they are not there already, then put them in place deliberately.

A positive mental attitude, plus good, strong and purposeful action, will equal total success every single time. That is powerful information that will bear repeating and affirming! *A positive attitude, plus a good strong purpose, will equal total success every single time!*

As that is the case you should be impelled into spending time improving your attitude and aligning your purpose. If your intention and reason for achieving a goal is strong enough, those attributes together will always make you win. Don't ever forget the simplicity of the formula . . . *determination is the common denominator with all success. You have to keep on keeping on. You Can Always Get What You Want . . . if you are determined to get it!*

I find this simplicity a most exciting experience. The knowledge that I can have whatever I want without compromising my reality of honesty and integrity, is absolutely exhilarating! You can get excited about those things too. Positively charge your desires with as much enthusiasm as possible, know who is in charge, and demand of yourself what you want from life.

Have faith in your own success and don't ever doubt yourself. Have faith in the SM. Have faith in Premier Imagination. Have faith in your goal and trust your abilities.

Faith is an important part of the formula

In fact, faith is a vital ingredient. When you set a goal you must have total faith in your ability to accomplish that task. Make the SM work positively for you, and have faith that it will succeed.

A light belief can have more desire, faith and emotion in it, than a heavy, laboured thought

The SM will accept a command no matter how light or wispy it may be. Passing thoughts and transitory desires will often amaze you when they transpire into fruition. What I am teaching you is how to control yourself for personal success, and that includes programming yourself in a very human way, so that such passing thoughts and transient desires become part of the success process, and not part of your downfall.

Eventually, every single thought that passes through your mind will be positive. That means you could decide to be in Australia for Christmas, and Brazil for the same Christmas. The two desires would fight themselves, and this is where single-mindedness comes into the equation.

Your positive attitude must be mixed with a gentle and giving single-mindedness. Definiteness, but not ruthlessness!

You cannot allow yourself to be blown off course by a slight breeze. How many people have given up the voyage of discovery with land in sight? Your success could be just around the corner, and it is this *sane single-mindedness* that will make you turn that corner and achieve your ambition.

You must also accept success as it is presented

to you. Was Columbus a failure because he didn't discover exactly what he was looking for? There are many ways to interpret success, and it is important that at no time do you punish yourself with an inability to accept success, or portions of it, as and when it comes your way.

Life will pay whatever price you ask of it!

If there is something you don't like about your life . . . change it. Demand to be in control of your thoughts and subsequently you will be in command of your actions. Use your mind power as a servant. Control it as you would command a computer.

You have urges in many different directions, and several varying aspects to your life. Can you imagine how you could accelerate your progress to success if these facets and directions were all channelled as energy into one goal? Naturally, this is not always totally feasible. You have to eat, you spend time with the family, you fix the gutters and check the engine oil, and so it goes on . . .

You can, however, take specific energy that is being misused or under-utilised, and channel it into helping you succeed. The sex urge is an important part of your existence. It is fun and vital to the continuation of the species. It is part of you . . . you may even be identified by your particular urge.

The truth is that the role of sex is connected to procreation and any deviation from that function is a curve, no matter how pleasurable. Most of us have two children. We probably need to have sex less than twenty times in our lives for sex to have fulfilled its purpose.

Channel this power into your drive for success

You can transfer this urge for sex, *without all of its physical ramifications and complications*, into your assault on success. Your partner would have to understand! Your spouse would have to be in agreement! I am talking essentially to those of you who have completed your family, but the principle and possibilities remain the same, in varying degrees, for every person on the planet.

Success is sexy!

The sex urge is tangible and readily understood by most of us. You can see that it is an incredibly powerful driving force. It motivates you to get things done. It pushes and prods you past the post when ordinarily you would have given up had the object not been sex. It encourages awareness of yourself and endows certain individuals with magnetism. This urge makes you attractive. It is one of life's major compelling forces!

This book is not about sex. I impart this data to you in order that you may explore possibilities with it. Such a challenge is not attractive to everyone, but it does work for some! Transmutation of the sex urge is possible and the option is available . . . the choice remains with you.

The human race will always be curious . . . we like to explore and reveal the secrets of the universe, we enjoy improving the quality of life, we demand to know how these bodies of ours really work . . . are we real? . . . is there life on other planets? Is the brain a thinking mind or something entirely different? There have been massive leaps forward recently in our knowledge of the brain, particularly its potential and capabilities, but most significantly for our purposes, how to inject into it knowledge that needs to be remembered. We now know that there are two sections to this organ, and one result of such research into left- and right-brain activity is to allow us to use both sections to full advantage! This of course is extremely helpful in anyone's quest for success.

The modern subject of *neurolinguistic programming* covers many aspects of human potential to bring about change within itself, and there are numerous books available on the subject. Richard Bandler and John Grinder pioneered NLP discoveries after studying the hypnotist Milton Erickson, and since these basic breakthroughs were made, many people have studied NLP and applied its philosophy to their own professions.

There is a book called *Accelerated Learning*, written by Colin Rose, and an organisation of the same name, which specialises in technology fundamentally connected to education, and has far more use than may at first be apparent. Whatever works for you in education can also benefit any mental situation where you need to feed information into your subconscious mind.

Bandler and Grinder established the importance of the three different ways to communicate with human beings. This became the basis of *neurolinguistic programming*.

Visual, auditory and kinaesthetic communication

Kinaesthetic simply means connected with bodily movement or action, and would include the sensations of touching and feeling.

The discovery of these forms of communication seems obvious, but let us briefly look at the implications and relevance to our assault on success. There is no point in trying to teach a visually oriented person with an audio tape, because it will not work as well as a video or live show. Action-oriented people would find data absorption easier if they were allowed to act it out. A video is not so relevant to a person with auditory orientation . . .

You have to inject yourself with data using the method most admissible to your sensory modus operandi. What is more acceptable to you . . . *seeing, hearing or acting*? Observe yourself and the way you see the world . . . discover your leaning and use it as a bias whenever you need to assimilate new information.

You can often tell what sense a person is most comfortable with by the way in which they communicate. Phrases such as '*I see what you mean*' or '*I get the picture*' can indicate a visual person. '*I hear what you are saying*' or '*that sounds stupid to me*' should tell you that this person leans towards the auditory. '*Feels good to me*' or '*give me a solid example*' shows a kinaesthetic approach to life.

Listen to yourself and discover your bias!

This new data can be used in sales. When you are selling a car to an auditory person, don't keep talking about how the car looks. You would say things like . . . '*Listen to the hi-fi, doesn't that sound beautiful?*' or '*Let's take a ride and hear how she sounds.*'

I acknowledge the advantage gained through knowledge of NLP in such sales-oriented situations, but I have no wish to trivialise the magnitude of this technology for such totally selfish ends. I am more interested in introducing you to this information as an aid to programming yourself for total success, *which must always include winning for others!* Find out what your leaning is and use it to full advantage in your quest for success . . . *just as a salesman might use it on you, but also using your additional knowledge of the 'win for all' ingredient!*

If you are a visual person, *see* your goals as already accomplished. If you are inclined to be auditory, *hear* the accomplishment, and listen to the applause and what people are saying about you . . . *'didn't he do well'* . . . *'I heard that it's the biggest selling record of all time.'* If you are primarily kinaesthetic, then *feel the ride of the car, hold on to that feeling of success, and give yourself a solid feeling of accomplishment.*

Another valuable technique available to you is called *anchoring*. In self-education, for instance, if you were to remember a time when you learnt something new and felt good about it, such as swimming or riding a bike, you would show the same physiological reactions as you did when you first experienced the learning. If you then touch your wrist or your shoulder, at the same time as remembering that experience, this touch will become *an anchor*.

In future, just by using the anchor (touching the shoulder or the wrist) you will be able to tap into the same enthusiasm and success that you initially felt. I call this . . .

Tuning in to the win!

If I am just about to take part in an important meeting, I firstly visualise mentally the desired outcome as already accomplished. I then *tune in to a win of a similar type from my past*.

In 1979, I had a major recording contract with one of the most successful labels in Britain. They let it be known that they were about to drop me. My manager and I parted company, and I felt generally demoralised and dejected . . . for a short while.

I decided that I would record a song written by someone else in an effort to rejuvenate my sagging career and refresh my involvement with the record company. I remembered a massive hit from the previous year and discovered who had written it. I recalled that person as having recorded at the same London studio that I used for an album a couple of years previously. I called the studio and got the telephone number of the partner of this person. I utilised the power of the record company I was still contracted to, and made it sound worth his while to be involved with me. Before this song was forthcoming, I arranged a meeting between the boss of the record company and the two partners.

The meeting occurred and I wasn't even mentioned. Instead, the partners were offered a £100,000 contract to produce one of the company's top groups. They turned the offer down for various career-oriented reasons, I pleaded for the song anyway, and eventually it was given to me. I realised that the owner of the record company relished any prospect of getting successful producers and songwriters involved with him. I decided to give him both! I took a cassette demo of the song up to the St John's Wood offices and studios, and decided to somehow reopen dialogue with him on the subject of *Phil Murray*.

He was in the studio mixing a new recording with one of his other groups. Will I ever forget the song he was mixing? I heard it so many times whilst waiting outside that studio door, *for more than three hours*. I wanted to eat, I wanted to drink, I needed the bathroom, but I fixed my attention on him and remained totally single-minded about the outcome of our meeting . . . which he didn't even know was about to occur.

Eventually he appeared in the doorway. *'I've got a hit song here, written by a hit songwriter, and produced by hit producers who I know you want to use . . . can I have three minutes of your time?'* I asked.

He led me into his office and listened to the cassette. I could see that he was excited, but I was still unaware of quite how that excitement would translate into positive impact on my future. He said that I could record the song anywhere in the world using any musicians I wished. It had worked! He walked with me through the record company offices telling all the staff, who previously had not returned my telephone calls, to give me whatever help I needed with the recording . . . *I was walking on air and living my dream*. I quickly called the producers, who had not *exactly* consented to produce me at this point, and got their agreement that they would do so.

We recorded the song, and although it wasn't a massive hit in its own right because of a change in distribution companies midway through its heaviest span of airplay, it found its way on to a compilation album which sold in excess of 250,000 copies.

I tune in to this episode of my life whenever I am 'trying to get something done'. I remember this success. I recall the feeling when I was told that I could record the song anywhere in the world. You will have periods in your life which can be a source of deep inspiration to you now. Spend some time on this exercise and discover similar motivational periods from your past!

Tune in to success, and remember the power of PI and the SM!

People were appalled when they discovered that a cinema in the United States had flashed subliminal messages on to the screen encouraging the audience to buy products available in the foyer. Their sales increased by up to 50%. The audience could not consciously see the messages because the flashes were too quick. The subconscious mind saw them, however, causing the audience to act according to what it had been told was good.

Use your Subconscious mind . . . it does as it is told. Be definite, do not get waylaid, and remember that determination is the common denominator of all success.

If you need to eliminate unwanted feelings and uncomfortable incidents from your memory, then you can utilise *the Zip formula.* I include such a tip in this book as it can help those of you who are hung up on incidents from the past. Many of us are fixated on memories, and whilst you are conscious of an unpleasant recollection, you are not aware of *the now*; whilst you are aware of an unwanted emotional nuance of memory, you are not concentrating on the plan for success. This is the opposite of my formula for tuning in to a win.

Living in history is a useless pastime, yet this diversion from the present reality is, I am afraid, one with which many people are obsessed! It is your choice of course, but you may never use the excuse *that your mind just wanders* or *you were just daydreaming.* Sorry . . . those days are over! A vital ingredient of success is an ability to control your mind. Concentrated mental compulsion will illuminate your path to the stars. Mental diversions can block that route!

If you seek sympathy for past hurt then you must

cease that unproductive desire and get yourself into *present time*, for it is here that you are able to control the future . . . *and the past*!

Mind Management is so relatively simple when compared with its opposite harmonic of mental anarchy! You are either controlled or in control . . . *and the choice is yours!*

Your ability to confront any memory will relate to your dominance over it. Whilst you are confronting any contents of this store of information, you can choose between being *the effect* of it, or *holding power* over it. Some Mind Management may be harder to exercise than I have so simplistically described, particularly if a person has not exerted any type of control over straggling and strangling thoughts up until this point. However, through a gradual process of *exerting will* this state of affairs will change.

The Zip process

The Zip process is simple. Allow the picture, incident or memory that is bothering you to come into your awareness. Look at it and listen to it. Experience the sensations within it . . . touch, feel, smell, motion, emotion, highs and lows. Mentally interact with this memory from beginning to end. View the detail and get into deep communication within. When you reach the end of this information chunk, and you are confident of having achieved a good level of mental communication with it, *Zip* through it from end to beginning, backwards, in reverse, *quickly*, in just a few seconds. The processing speed of the SM is phenomenally rapid and it will be quite able to reverse-read at this speed. You will swiftly become familiar with this process . . . especially when you discover that it works! To eliminate more stubborn unwanted feelings still trapped within the memory, whilst Zipping, try the ridiculous by perhaps adding a soundtrack of circus music, or dubbing it with some zany special effects.

Communicate, familiarise, mentally relive the experience as it was . . . then Zip through it backwards in just a few seconds. This will wipe out the uncomfortable concepts from this memory . . . yet the picture *without* the unwanted emotion will remain. Zipping is a process which works well! It is a procedure which facilitates control and places you firmly in a state of Mind Management over your memories. The SM will understand this fast Zip backwards. The SM works at a remarkable speed.

Zipping is simple. Do not complicate it!

I also utilise a technique which I call . . .

Pinpointing

I first used this trick when I began performing in large venues back in 1976. Up until that time I had mainly played small clubs, where audiences were continuously visible to the performer. Suddenly I was singing in a band who were playing City Halls and ballrooms. It was a quick progression and a big step up the ladder. However, I found myself only performing to the first few rows of the audience, and alienating those people whom I couldn't see because of the bright lights shining in my eyes.

After exploring different possibilities to remedy this shortcoming, and trying various cures for this common performance deficiency, I discovered my ability to *Pinpoint*.

This involved a mental orientation of myself within the venue. I would *Pinpoint* the corners of the auditorium in front of me, and when I had located them physically with my eyes, if possible, or mentally if not, I would perform the same exercise for the corners behind me. It seemed that once I had performed the Pinpointing operation, this simple procedure enabled my communications to travel to the extremities of the venue . . . as far as my Pinpoints.

You can project as far as you can see . . . mentally

I perfected this trick during a six-week European tour of gigantic venues, which included sports arenas and huge municipal complexes. That tour was in 1977, and we ended it by playing the Reading Festival.

We were backstage until it was our time to play. When we hit the stage there were thirty thousand people looking at us. An audience stretching farther than my eyes could see. I began the Pinpointing process, but I was in the open air and there were no corners to Pinpoint as had become my habit. I was disoriented. Before I could find a solution to this problem, we began the first number. Just about everything you could imagine went wrong in that first song.

Perhaps we all had the same Pinpointing problem . . . the song was out of time, we stopped after the instrumental introduction and tried to regain the correct tempo, none of the band could hear properly, we struggled to communicate with each other, I pulled the microphone from its stand, but the plug was faulty and not connected properly and consequently the microphone cable disengaged and left me inaudible. When the microphone was fixed, my knees began to knock together . . . literally. This had never happened before, and has not since.

We had played the first five songs of our set before I was able to get a bearing on the back of the audience, who by this time were thoroughly uninterested. We didn't ever discuss that performance, as I believe we were so deeply embarrassed by the experience.

I now use Pinpointing in meetings. It helps me orientate myself within a room. It stabilises me in an unusual environment, and gives me a feeling of strength in uncommon surroundings. *It is invaluable when speaking in public!*

Pinpointing is a trick which you can utilise.

Now is the time to remind yourself who is in charge, whilst checking your blueprint for success. Get healthy both mentally and physically. Rid yourself of bad and unwanted habits. Tune in to success, determination and definiteness, making sure that you have at least one *principle-centred, long-term goal*.

STAGE SIX

Principle-centred, long-term goals

'Total success is the continuing involvement in the pursuit of a worthy ideal, which is being realised for the benefits of others rather than at their expense' Dennis Waitley

There is no mystery about goal-setting. A goal is not something that must have an intrinsic divine comportment; it is not essential for a goal to have a Spiritual Master in the ether waves. Goals rarely descend on you from elsewhere to dominate over your beingness, and seldom seek you out for their own ends. A goal is a desire that needs a human instigative presence.

You have to compose your own goals!

You have to take mental responsibility before the beginning of any physical achievement. Throughout the ages there have been men and women who believed their destiny was the caprice of another. Such sentiment has often been the instigator of indolence. We know of many stories from great men and women who spoke of their goals in life being allotted to them by a *higher being*. I fully believe in many of these phenomena and wouldn't ever deny such possibilities. What I am saying to you is this . . . don't sit around waiting for the call.

There is no excuse for an absence of goals!

A goal can be small- or medium-size, long- or short-term, huge, divine, spiritual, worldly, small-minded or even someone else's. Anything can be a goal. I know something else for sure . . . every single person reading these words has set at least one goal for themselves. You bought this book and you are reading it . . . unless you just borrowed it because you had not *set the goal of owning it for yourself*.

Reading a book on success is a time-wasting distraction if you do not practise your newly acquired knowledge expediently. I was browsing through the Psychology, Inspirational and Motivational section of a major bookstore not so long ago, when a fellow browser commented to me that someone should write a book called *How To Wean Yourself Off Motivational Books*, and I very nearly took this advice and wrote it! Many people get high on the success stories of others without administering the principles that produced such success into their own lives.

It is an easy mistake and one which you should scrupulously check yourself for!

I know that many people viewed much of their early education as irrelevant, *because they had no intention of using that specific information in their postulated future*. Yet every small piece of data that you assimilate has a bearing of some description on your expectations, and specific knowledge can have indirect positive consequences in addition to any direct and obvious effects. Bear this in mind if your mature, self- educational outlook is somewhat negative. Remember that *knowledge is wisdom*, and that such a state will afford you an inner guidance system that will accelerate your mission for success. Treasure each piece of newly discovered knowledge and utilise it fully.

When I was at school, the dominant viewpoint on foreign languages seemed to be that learning Latin was a waste of time. German, French and Spanish were endowed with a far more practical usefulness by the educational establishment, and consequently I studied German and French. We were advised that dead languages should be avoided, and the Latin class struggled to attract three pupils. Only the direct consequences of study were allowed into this equation. The longer-term and somewhat healthier viewpoint *on general educational qualities*, which it is essential to embrace if we are to prosper, is far more relevant than may seem immediately apparent.

I subsequently discovered that Latin was alive and well in just about every aspect of the English language. I cannot think of any scholastic subject that would have been more helpful to me as an author, than a good, even basic, grounding in Latin.

You may not be consciously aware of yourself utilising freshly acquired knowledge. Your *successful use of knowledge* may not at first be blatantly apparent, but you can rest assured that demonstrated in your everyday life is precisely what you have studied, assimilated and believed.

If you read garbage newspapers that espouse bigoted viewpoints and gossip, then you may expect such inflow to reflect into your life. If your friends demonstrate negative viewpoints and you are frequently in contact with them, be certain that their pessimism will scrape away at your positivity. If the people around you have low expectations of life, if your environment is down-tone, if your dress is sloppy, if your body is unwashed, if your job is depressing, if your spouse is antagonistic . . . *do not expect a whirlwind of success to whoosh in your direction!*

It is your duty as an Advanced PAC Practitioner to surround yourself with inspiration and beauty, quality and craftsmanship, classic and mighty aesthetic appeal, poetry and lyric, music and the sound of silence, TTM and TFT, knowledge of the SM and CM, Premier Imagination and Secondary Imagination.

Surround yourself with great ideas!

Check your Supergroup for positive charge and eliminate any negativity that may have crept in through the back door. Give your family an optimism perusal and offer assistance to help them stay on the bright side of life.

Never, ever, ever, ever compromise with what is real and right to a just, honourable and creative way of thinking!

You've all set goals. Deciding to eat in a certain restaurant someday is setting a goal. Deciding on the size of your family is goal-setting.

You must acknowledge the power of goal-setting!

Can you imagine how damaging it would be for you to set the wrong goal for yourself? We need to look at this subject carefully so that we may use this powerful goal technology to its fullest benefit.

Of course I am taking for granted the fact that, whoever you are or whatever you think you are, you must be aspiring towards a better quality of life. Any person who even contemplates improvement for any aspect of their existence has already begun to climb the ladder of success. It is often helpful to thoroughly acknowledge yourself for taking such steps towards achieving your own personal success, no matter how small or apparently insignificant those steps may seem. Pat yourself on the back, congratulate yourself, throw a party, welcome yourself to the real big time, reward yourself. I mean it . . . do all or any of those things. Talk to yourself now, and get excited about the future. Write fifty lines that say '*I thank myself for my success!*'

I have read various reports that seem to put anyone who has a goal, and a plan for the accomplishment of that goal, into the top 2% of the population who are likely to achieve personal success.

Develop a nostalgia for the future!

Forget about the past . . . it has disappeared and will never return. Experience excitement about your successful future as if it already exists in the exact format you desire most. Can you accept that by mapping out your life right now, and stating what you intend to accomplish with your plan, you put yourself into that top 2%?

Can you statistically afford not to map out your life?

A ship without a course; an explorer without a compass; a city without a map! Are you driftwood, or a powerful speed boat heading for a port in paradise? The choice is and will always be . . . yours!

There are leaders and followers. Always remember that leaders are answerable to their commanders, too. Neither one category is necessarily senior to the other. Your goal can be connected to either division. It seems that followers can expect less financial reward than their leaders, but I cannot see how we could have leaders without anyone to lead, and it is purely a matter of role rather than hierarchy. Decide if your goal is in leadership or not, and be happy about falling into either classification.

Using a pen and paper or word processor, compose a succinct sentence on the one major personal intention that you feel is within you, awaiting manifestation into your physical life. Do not refer to anything other than inner knowingness. *Trust yourself and do not contemplate or second guess the reactions of others to your new way of embracing and utilising this formula for success.* Don't feel that you are '*too big for your boots*' if you set what up until now has seemed too high a target for yourself. This exercise will cost you nothing, and can give you a massive boost in your quest for progress.

If a genie manifested from nowhere and agreed to grant you one personal wish . . . what would you ask for? Write down your answer and accept it.

If you have an answer written down on paper, that will be a help to you. If you have been unable to provide yourself with just this one answer to the exclusion of all other intentions, that does not pose a problem. Not everyone has just one goal that they want to achieve within their lifetime . . . or to put it another way, *one magnificent obsession*! At the very least I want you to write down a few things that you would like to achieve within your lifetime.

If you cannot find that one burning ambition, then write down whatever it is you would rather do than something else.

If you have anything written down on that paper, then you should feel good about yourself. This is powerful personal information and, using it as such, I suggest that you predict the sentiments as self-fulfilling prophecies. This of course does not mean that you now sit back and wait for the goal to self-fulfil. You must play an active part in any accomplishment.

Now you need a plan for the realisation of your goal. A step-by-step guide towards self-satisfaction. Who do you need to meet? What information do you need? What, where, who and how?

My goals have incorporated songs and singing ever since I was seven years old. I remember creating the outline plan for a musical play just before I went to sleep one night. I shouted to my mother and told her all about it. That concept was complete with staging ideas, songs and performers. I progressed to a tape recorder and produced my own programmes. My imagination worked well for me, occasionally it dominated me, but I was always aware of the delineation between physical and mental reality.

When I was sixteen, I helped form a band, and began writing my first songs in earnest. In 1972 I remember being asked in a local magazine interview what my ambition was. I said that my goal was to record at Trident Studios in London. Lots of music that I admired had been recorded there, and it was an extremely successful studio, although sadly it is no longer in existence.

In 1973, I remember going to see David Bowie at Newcastle City Hall. Before Bowie hit the stage, the Spiders from Mars appeared. The drummer sat at the kit holding a stick on each of his tom toms and stared straight at the audience, like a being from outer space. The Spiders looked terrific. I turned to my girlfriend, now my wife, and told her that someday I would play with those musicians . . . especially the drummer.

They were at the peak of their world popularity at the time, and I was the singer in a local group, mainly playing social clubs and using other people's songs. In 1975, my guitarist friend called me excitedly and asked me to visit him for a chat. He had recorded an album with his other band, which unfortunately had not sold well, but had been heard and appreciated by the Spiders from Mars . . . they were looking for a new guitarist and had asked him to join. What should he do? He asked me, because if he were to leave our band it would place us in the awkward position of having to find a replacement as good as him at short notice.

I told him to join as quickly as possible, which he did. They recorded an album and toured, but went the way of most groups and split in 1976. I was living in London by that time, but had returned to the north east for a weekend break. I bumped into my friend as soon as I arrived, and he asked if the drummer from the Spiders had called me, as he was looking for a singer to form a new band with.

I remembered my goal and got that excited feeling in my stomach. He hadn't called, so I telephoned him . . . that night! Following that call, I travelled back down south to London overnight, then onwards to East Grinstead the next morning. The drummer and I talked, we played, and the band was formed immediately with three other members. We made our first recordings at . . . guess where? . . . Trident Studios, London. We then toured and recorded an album. We became the best of friends. Just prior to another tour, which was to include several cities in Europe supporting a big-name band, we discovered that this group were seeking a new bass player. The job went to the original Spiders bass player. We then toured together for six weeks.

When we returned to East Grinstead, the original Spiders guitarist visited. We were playing in London the following night and the bass player and guitarist were coming to the gig. All three of them in one place, and guess what happened? *We didn't play together!*

That goal had become an epitome of the self-fulfilling prophecy philosophy . . . with an energy all of its own. When the time arrived for it to reach its climax, my interest had diminished. My new goals of writing and performing successful songs had taken precedence. It was, however, of more than a passing interest to me when I saw just how far that goal progressed, seemingly of its own accord.

You can change your goal

The goal isn't sacred. The goal is a tool. Use it for your own selfish aims, but always in the service of others. Use it for the betterment of mankind. Utilise it to give or to get, but whatever you do, use it practically! This goal technology works . . . other people are using it daily and getting amazing results, so why shouldn't you?

I want to talk about happiness. I have questioned many people about their goals, and the desire for happiness always seems to be present in some form or another. Often it is the main goal, and a worthy ideal it surely is!

The problem with happiness is that it seems to

present itself as a by-product of another aspiration. If you are seeking happiness itself, then what exactly is it? Where is it?

Happiness is achieved during the execution of an otherwise unrelated goal, in direct proportion to accomplishment and the fulfilment of purpose.

It seems that it is not an end point in itself. Rather, it is an emotion which gathers momentum from the energy of your participation in other activities. You feel happiness when you are doing whatever it is that you feel you should be doing. When you are engaged with something you do not want to do, it seems that unhappiness is the dominant emotion. You cannot *do* happiness . . . you have to engage yourself in other activities for it to manifest as an emotion. *Accept happiness as a by-product.*

If you desire money from a goal then that yearning must include service as an intrinsic ingredient. If your goal is to travel I can't see money forthcoming, unless you qualify that travel with some kind of service, for example writing, courier work or war correspondent.

Choose your goals wisely

Goals can be a part of your life for a long time, as my previous example has illustrated. If you have not honed the finer points and the goal has rough edges, then be prepared for exactly what you have ill-planned to arrive into your life. Your subconscious mind will strive to deliver exactly what you told it you wanted!

We moved to America for a time, and then returned to our native north east of England for a couple of years. We worked so hard, and really felt as though we were becoming a little too divorced from our spiritual leanings than we cared to admit at the time. We decided to move back to the East Grinstead area where I had lived since 1976, and consequently bought a house in Felbridge, Surrey. All the time we were living away from this area, whenever we had difficulties in business we used to say to each other, '*What would our friend Jay do in this situation?*' This eased our attention from our immediate difficulties, and also allowed us to use his viewpoint . . . or his potential viewpoint as we were able to interpret it. We took someone else on board at no extra cost.

Just prior to our return south, we were confident about the future and felt that Jay possessed the qualities necessary for the speedy fulfilment of our business aspirations. *He would have the answers. Jay would get the ball rolling.*

We had looked after his daughter when my wife and I first lived together in the late seventies, and he had been the minister who married us in 1980. It was Jay whom I bumped into at the new-year-plus-one party in 1993, and it was Jay who reminded me of goals and targets. It was this same person who introduced me to a whole host of new and very positive information sources. The business took on a new momentum!

I thought that if this friend of mine could inspire me that far, then he was sure to be a source of yet further motivation . . . and so he was. He introduced me to a Brian Tracy programme called *The Psychology of Success*. I then borrowed from him the Anthony Robbins book, *Ultimate Power*. I later purchased it, together with many other titles that showed themselves as potential inspirers!

You Can Always Get What You Want was conceived, and I began outlining early ideas which culminated in a synthesis of technology of which

I was already cognisant, with new knowledge that I was still assimilating.

Jay introduced me to Maxwell Maltz's *Psycho Cybernetics, Accelerated Learning and Neuro Linguistic Programming*. I then read Dale Carnegie's *How to Win Friends and Influence People*.

Meanwhile, I was working, and my business was gaining momentum. I went to Jay's American Independence Day party, he told me about Napoleon Hill, and I bought myself a copy of *Think and Grow Rich*. From these beginnings I went on to discover Shakti Gawain, Steven Covey, Shad Helmstetter, Dennis Waitley and Wayne Dyer. There are many people out there discovering and writing about powerful, life-improving technologies for the benefit of us human beings. And of course there are still the powerful teachings from the old religions and esoteric sources.

During my research for this book, I embarked upon a sideline venture to discover the basic and earliest personal development work which could lay claim to being the inspiration behind this modern movement I now find myself engaged with. Claude Bristol's *The Magic of Believing*, and *TNT: The Power Within*, which he wrote with Harold Sherman, helped orientate me. The more modern writings of old-established sentiments by Shakti Gawain, such as *Creative Visualisation* and *The Path of Transformation*, reminded me of the spiritual aspect . . . and then I discovered a very small book by James Allen called *As a Man Thinketh*, the title taken from an aphorism which I have also seen in the Bible. As far as I can ascertain, this book was written more than one hundred years ago, and illustrated sentiments which I had found in more than one subsequent volume of like-minded work.

James Allen concentrated in a very poetic format on the power of thought, and the duty of every human being to contemplate life with purity. I recommend this book, and felt satisfied for some time that I had discovered the goal of my sideline venture.

On reflection, and as a further note to this new edition, I feel there is no work that can really lay claim to be the inspirational source of man's constant quest for self-improvement. The Bible and Buddhist writings contain most of the revelations and motivational ideas that now dominate modern life for many of us. Madame Blavatsky, in her nineteenth-century work which included *The Secret Doctrine*, laid bare much knowledge which until that time had been reserved for the assimilation of initiates only . . . *it was felt to be so forceful!*

Alice Bailey wrote a most powerful set of books in the 1920s, 1930s and 1940s, which uncovered mysteries of life little contemplated before. The datum that *energy follows thought* was popularised through these writings, which are perhaps the most significant and complete treatments of cosmic existence that have ever been written.

Telepathy, altruism, philanthropy and human beingness are all subjects intrinsically related to true, modern success. These themes can all be traced to works represented by the Theosophical Society and the Lucis Trust in some way, shape or form, as well as many ancient and esoteric works which are not widely available for public scrutiny.

The point of me relating this to you . . . we expected Jay to help us, and even had half a plan for getting him interested in the music business. The help we expected came from him, and we were quick to realise it had taken on a form other than what had been expected. We had got exactly what we had decided we would get. We took all that came with open arms and heaps of gratitude. Jay's indirect input into our lives was precious and more beneficial than any direct relationship.

Look out for the curve!

You may have planned well and worked hard, expecting a return from a certain place and in a particular fashion. Your dreams *will* be answered, but in a form perhaps not as obvious or blatant as you would expect. *Be determined yet flexible*. There are many paradoxes in the field of human behavioural improvement. There are those who believe in a Supreme Being who has everything mapped out for you, but that you still have self-determination and the ability to change events. You must decide for yourself on the subject of paradoxes.

Paradoxical situations always run the risk of ridiculing any subject, most of all a subject as sensitive as *the human being*. If you predict success for yourself in a given field, with massive amounts of money as a by-product of your service, you have to accept that the financial reward could come from anywhere. *You could even win the premium bonds or the football pools!*

I must also urge you at this point, while we are talking about personal success, earning truck loads of money, and extracting from life exactly what we want from it, to pay close attention to the simple axiom already mentioned and hinted at throughout this book . . . no matter how you approach life, there is no greater service than that quality of giving to others, therefore . . .

It is impossible to be a great giver and also to be unsuccessful in life!

How do you like that one? It is an immutable law of the universe which states that *what you give you get*.

When you give, a vacuum is created. That vacuum has to be filled. What you put out, you have to get back. *Nature does not tolerate vacuum!*

Plant good seed . . . what you harvest will reflect exactly what you have sown!

There is no reason at all why any goal cannot contain honesty, integrity and a 'win for all' ingredient. In any situation, no matter what it is, there is a formula in there somewhere allowing all parties to win. If your goal contains this 'win for all' ingredient, whatever it may be, then you have the force of good on your side. I am not saying that you cannot win without someone else winning. We all know only too well that this is so. In fact the *I win . . . you lose* formula has been the trend for most of history. As we experience the beginnings of this New Age of Aquarius, it is apparent that new ways of thinking are essential for the human race. There is a shallow-win formula, and a deep-win formula. You have the choice of paths. I suggest that the 'win for all' ingredient will be one of the most potent factors in determining success for future business and interpersonal achievement.

A mission statement can assist you

When you write out on paper the exact nature of your life's mission, or main *reason for being*, it will tell you a lot about yourself. This is another tool which I heartily recommend. You may align your daily decisions with your long-term Mission Statement and formulate conclusions based on integrity which you have preconceived. A *Personal Mission Statement*, or PMS, is a valuable document. Every true Advanced PAC member has Mission Statements . . . both Personal and Business (BMS), and also Family (FMS), and Hobby (HS). That is a minimum of four Mission Statements.

If you have not already compiled your four Mission Statements, then now is the time to do it.

Your PMS should be exactly that . . . *personal*, a verbal connection with *you*. What *you* are going to do in life. The influence *you* aim to have on society. Everything to do with *you*.

I share my PMS with you in the hope that it will be both inspirational and directional. Use it as a guideline until you are more confident working with this technology alone. *The Mission Statement itself should be your total aspiration contained in one succinct sentence.* This can take some time to compose, and I advise you to address it as a medium- to long-term venture, redrafting as many times as necessary to achieve the complete and polished end product. Treat this statement as a work of art and respect its significance in your life. Practise composition and allow your inner feelings to guide the substance and general trend of the sentence.

A *Visualisation Statement* should follow your main declaration. In this section you may set down on paper exactly how you would like your life to progress in relation to your Mission Statement. Ideal scenarios and practicalities can be embraced under this category. This Visualisation portion of the statement, by its very nature, will be constantly changing, and at no time should any aspect of the Mission

Tool take precedence over you and any new ideals that may have entered into your life. The world is a cyclic environment, and this has a direct bearing on the thoughts of the human mind contained in every sentient body. You must warm to your own instincts and treat tools as what they are . . . assistance!

I always compose in the present tense, as if what I want to occur is already happening. I align the value of personal affirmations closely with my Personal Visualisation Statement, which in turn is a reflection and harmonic of the Main Mission Statement.

Personal Mission Statement

Using the medium of entertainment, I am dedicated to the act of providing enjoyment, increasing awareness, and learning to appreciate the natural talent that lies within both myself and others.

Visualisation Statement

1
I write quality songs, plays, novels, articles, success literature and inspirational material

2
I record quality songs and inspirational material

3
I research and write success formulae
and goal techniques

4
I am an excellent live performer

5
I have an expanding audience

6
I build as a vehicle for myself and others

7
I have respectful recognition within the
entertainment and personal development industries

8
My work as a writer, singer, songwriter and
producer, sells well around the world

9
I am known as an artiste
of quality and integrity

10
I am a good actor

11
I write stories and plays that people enjoy

12
I am a successful person

13
I am a strong family man

14
I am a good husband and father

15
I enjoy life to the full

Personal affirmations

I am wealthy
I am successful
I earn in excess of £100,000 per year
I earn this money from many enjoyable sources
People like my work
I am popular
I am good at my job
I am a good father
I am a good husband
I always have time for my family
I always have time for my friends
I have a second home in Florida
I own two new cars
My wife does not need to work
I give lots of money to charity
I always keep 10% of my income
My income is always increasing
I adore being rich
Being rich allows me to be more spiritual
I am constantly improving myself spiritually
I like myself, I like myself, I like myself

Your BMS is a concise statement of intentions connected with your business. I know of businesses that have, at the base of their modus operandi, the one desire to increase the asset base of the

owners. A BMS is a little more complicated than a PMS
. . . because it has more involvement with other people.

*A narrow-minded admiral is more likely to incite
mutiny than a caring captain. How to avoid a
rough passage . . .*

You may well technically own the business completely,
but to the degree that other people are helping with
its continued success, then they have a stake also.
Employees and their families, suppliers, retailers,
wholesalers, and the public, all of these people have
to be included in the aims and aspirations of any
business! You have to include them all in your
BMS. If you wish to avoid the *'I just do as I'm
told'* attitude . . . *'more than my job's worth'* . . . *'it's
not worth my while'* . . . *'that isn't my job'* . . . *'you've
got the wrong department'* . . . *'sorry I can't help . . .
and I don't know who can!'* . . . then get your BMS
honed finely. Show everyone that you care, then
increase the level of that care! Everyone connected
with your business has to win for it to be truly
successful!

When I work in studios on projects that are dear
to my heart, and I see that there is a youngster
on work experience in the building, I always invite
them in while I am working. I think of how I
would have felt at their age to be in their situation,
and I share as much of my knowledge with them
as I think it is fair to expect them to assimilate.
The particular studio may not belong to me, these
people are not on work experience with me, but
they are part of my BMS. *If they will accept . . . then
I will give.*

If your BMS is honourable, then without a shadow of a doubt that fact alone at the base of your modus operandi will place your business ahead of others who have chosen less honourable and more self-ish aims.

Think of everyone connected with your business, and compose your Business Mission Statement around them and preferably with them.

I share with you the Mission Statement for my company.

PeRFECT WORDS and MUSIC Limited

Mission Statement

Through publishing, recording and live performance, we are dedicated to the service of quality works and artistes, with the aim of enjoyment and enhancement for the world as a whole, whilst improving the fortune, and excellence of life, for everyone concerned with PeRFECT WORDS and MUSIC.

Visualisation Statement

1
We honestly and successfully market quality works and artistes . . . worldwide

2
We provide a secure and enjoyable working environment for all employees

3
We always view situations long term

4
We never ever take short cuts to the detriment of a product

5
We are seen as an honest and successful company in the entertainment industry

6
We are involved in many aspects of the entertainment and personal development industries

7
We are innovative

8
We are helpful to others within the same industry

9
We are wealthy market leaders

10
We maintain dignity at all time

An FMS must likewise reflect the needs and aspirations of your complete family. For that reason alone, it will need to be a group composition. Harmonious and successful living will be achieved far more quickly and easily, with an aligned Family Mission Statement that has been written by the whole family.

The Murray family Mission Statement

We provide a loving and secure environment, both physically and spiritually, where the individual can feel comfortable as a creative and gnostic being, whilst learning the skills required for accomplishment and enjoyment in life.

Visualisation statement

1
We love each other as best friends

2
We listen to each other with interest

3
We are kind to one another

4
We always have time for each other

5
We have fun

6
We learn from each other

7
We live in a creative environment

8
We are creative as a family

9
We play together

10
We achieve a high level of education

11
We travel the world

12
We experience new things together

13
We are successful as a family

14
We are wealthier every day in every way

You may also want an Extended Supergroup Mission Statement. Discuss this possibility with the other members and seek agreement. I am convinced that it will inspire you all, and for the short time that it will take to compose, it will pay you back a thousand fold. My fourth Mission Statement is for the PAC, and can be seen towards the end of this book.

The technology that I am discovering and sharing with you is at the very heart of life itself. It will produce very strong individuals . . . but the strongest of you all will be those that learn the art of *interdependence*.

You can be independent and interdependent without hypocrisy

Interdependence is a concept which includes the 'win for all' sentiment. It has replaced rivalry as a popular philosophy and concentrates on working together. Giving to others is included as a basic quality within its wider theory.

You can interdepend and profit from one another!

Interdependence is not the art of taking, but the skill of giving to others, and accepting the return when it arrives. If you have set up a business that involves interdepartmental rivalry, can you honestly sit down and tell me, especially after reading this book, that this rivalry is a healthy alternative to mutually co-operative methods? Where there is rivalry, there is duplicity. Where there is duplicity, there is a down- tone environment. Where this attitude prevails, true achievers do not go.

True achievers have peace of mind as a fulcrum. They balance themselves, and if they feel at any time that they have dropped beneath the sight of their original horizons, they will depart for healthier pastures. Part of their success formula includes inner happiness. Achievement in the physical world is part of that, but not the greater part.

If you want success, then it is wise to have successful people around you. For this to happen, you have to create a desirable environment. If it is duplicitous, you will attract people who enjoy that atmosphere, and those people will not be the most conducive to your own success.

You need to create a true interdependent situation within a happy environment. Good cycles of communication have to be adopted as the norm. You have to be able to share time with your colleagues. There is little that can make a human being feel worse than feelings of uselessness, insignificance and inferiority.

This data is valuable for any aspect of life. When you have listened to someone, let them know that you are interested in their communication by asking a question about what has just been said. Ask about a certain aspect of a particular point. This will also help you to become a true listener. Leave a respectful communication gap before delivering your response. Ensure that your reply illustrates a complete understanding of what has just been said. Do not interrupt!

You will be astounded by the effect this has on the people around you. In his time, Dale Carnegie was reputed to have been an incredible conversationalist, *because of his ability to sit and listen with interest*. This is an important practice to add to your list of attributes as an Advanced PAC Practitioner.

Using a person's name is a powerful tool. People like to be known by their name. It is a *button* of our time to be thought of as a number. You can show how important a person is to you by using their name. It has a magical impact. Physical contact can also establish good rapport. A warm handshake and a *'hello . . . first name,'* where appropriate, is obvious, yet so many people don't do it.

Advanced PAC Practitioners make it their business to know the finer details of a colleague's likes and dislikes. When you remember the birthday of the daughter of an employee, and you send her a card, you can imagine the impact this one small action has on that person's life. Can you see how this will help you?

How often do you *compliment* the people around you? Can you see the value of a compliment? I am not suggesting for one moment that your new life has to be filled with flattery, lies and cheap tricks.

I guarantee you this . . . you need never lie when giving compliments. *Find out what you like about someone and focus on that point*. Every living person has some good quality about them. As you become well versed in the ways of *positivity*, focusing on the good will become more automatic. Always compliment truthfully!

If you have employees who continually *get it wrong*, there will always be something that they do well. Continue to compliment the points that they do well. Those people will do everything in their power to get all the minus points up to the quality of their good points . . . because you have given them *motivation*.

People like to please people

You are surrounded by allies. Always present them with reasons to like you even more. Genuineness will be natural to PAC Practitioners who are truly cognisant of this condition of *positivity* that they aspire towards on a continual basis. Your communication skills are a direct reflection of your *state of being*.

You cannot deliver a tirade to your workforce and expect them to feel good about you. You can't show temper and preach peace. You dare not be seen as duplicitous whilst advocating the theories and practices of my book. People in glass houses should not throw stones. Exude the right formula and expect good results. *You get what you give*, yet the modern slant to that ancient aphorism is to *give as good as you get*.

No no no! If you are not satisfied with what you

get, *give some more*. PAC people do not depend on the weather for their moods.

Advanced PAC Practitioners make their own weather!

You are the Creator. You are the Source Point. You are numero uno, top of the class, head of the queue, leading the league, first in the table. To be those things you have to *make your own weather!*

That translates into everyday life like this . . . no one can ever make you what you don't want to be. Your mood is not dependent on external stimuli. Your quality of communication is not based on the incoming calibre of confabulation. You are a PAC member, and this is a basic essential of Advanced Practice. You have two ears, and one mouth . . . that should help you remember what ratio of listening to talking you should aim for.

I attended a very good grammar school, where it was cool to be rebellious. Two ingredients of that insurrection were smoking and foul language. In the subject of the latter I excelled. I was able to cut a swot down to size at twenty paces. I carved a niche for myself as Head of the *new language school*. We only spoke in obscenities, and anyone using inoffensive language was immediately punished for being obsequious.

One of the basic tenets of my new school was the practical point that this new language had to be used regularly. Once we had devised a new vulgar profanity, it would then have to be employed immediately, preferably on someone to whom it would cause maximum offence.

When this offence was apparent, I would then get the victims to place their hands over their mouths, and get them to say this latest blasphemous creation that had upset them. If they were soft enough to do this, I would say something puerile like . . . *'See, words don't hurt do they?'*

Words can hurt!

Words are designed to convey a meaning, and as a sentiment medium, they can hurt. You must choose your words wisely, and always remember that the subconscious mind translates words literally, and never poetically, lyrically, beautifully, or metaphorically . . . *literally! The subconscious mind translates words literally.*

Confession is powerful therapy and involves being listened to. As the ability to listen increases, the skill of hearing exactly what is being said grows. *This means duplicating communication as it is intended, and not as interpreted.*

The game of Chinese Whispers is not such an unusual analogy of real-life communication as you may first imagine. The game involves a circle of people, and the first person whispers something like . . . *'I know a game where everyone wins and the game is simply life.'* By the time it reaches the last person it has become . . . *'If it's all the same I love to sin and I don't mean with my wife.'*

Communication breakdowns can be repaired by resuming communication. Stalemate is the worst business or personal situation you can ever find yourself regretting. Avoid not speaking, dodge no dialogue and avert sealed lips! If personal communication is prohibited, you begin to rely on the third party.

The power of the third party is wicked!

When you hear from a third party that someone has said something about you that is derogatory, the power of that disparaging information is multiplied forcefully. It follows that if your best friend recommends a Phil Murray album to you, then chances are higher of you both getting a copy, and enjoying it. The third party can interfere with good judgement. Keep your lines of communication clean. Don't listen to gossip. Gossip is another word for garbage. Demand good sources of information. Exact rumour-free dialogue from your colleagues.

Do not speak disparagingly of even your worst enemy

Work at having your enemies as good friends. There is always a potential desire and method, no matter how unlikely that seems. Meanwhile, don't let anyone know of any disagreements you have with anyone, and don't ever expect a third party to repair a relationship for you. Meet these situations head on and confront your new life personally. Remember that others are listening to you, and most people understand the simple principle that if you speak about someone else in a certain way, then chances are you will speak about them in the same way. Don't say unkind things about anyone.

Right thinking + right speaking + right doing = right being

A mediator is in a powerful position. If there is ever a time in your life when you feel there is no alternative but to use such a person, then choose wisely.

Beware of rumour mongers!

The act of communicating in parallels and parables can make an otherwise unpalatable communication tolerable. If you need to chastise someone, then you would be wise to show, by example in others, where they went wrong. Let them understand for themselves what happened. Let them tell you.

You can't ever gain altitude or respect by demanding them. These two honours are awarded to you by others, and your methods of communication will contribute greatly towards these awards coming sooner rather than later . . . or worse still, not at all.

You can live a life of quick fixes, with lots of short- term wins, and plenty of activity. But for ultimate success, as well as quick fixes, you have to have long-term goals which have an intrinsic ingredient of good principles. When all the quick fixes are over, you will still be there. When all the *fast friends* have departed for so-called faster and more exciting quick fixes, unless you are with them, you will still have to deal with yourself.

You need a blueprint. A plan is compulsory. You have to work towards the fulfilment of a goal to achieve any degree of happiness. A purpose for living is a necessity.

I often ask people in my profession about their

goals. The most prevalent reply that I get is *'I just want to be famous!'* I call this the *malaiseyness* symptom of our age. The striving for fame! Fame has become the end product . . . and yet fame is not really an accomplishment. The playing of the piano is the achievement. Fame is the by-product. The writing of the song is the feat. Fame is the consequence. Too many people see fame as a beingness.

We applaud fame and ignore talent

We have meteorologists starring in theatrical productions. The weather girl can fill a theatre because people have seen her on the television presenting a weather forecast! The radio disc jockey is more 'castable' than the graduate of stage school. The book written by the wife of a serial killer is more desirable to many people than the novel that has just won the Booker Prize. A page three girl from a newspaper can sell out a major tour . . . but the local band who write and rehearse every day of their lives because that is their purpose, cannot get coverage in their local newspaper.

We have to see the aspiration for talent as an applaudable strength. We must encourage the gathering of skill. We should reward the ambition of achievement. We can subsidise the weak in their struggle for genuine competence.

Skill, adeptness, deftness, dexterity, mastery, proficiency, ability, capacity, talent, faculty and craft, in any human undertaking, are all commendable qualities that far exceed the importance of fame. *Murderers are famous. Anyone can become famous! Don't just strive for fame!*

You are in a position to choose your goals. Why not

choose big goals? Why not choose honesty and integrity as intrinsic qualities for your goals? Give yourself the challenge of finding the 'win for all' ingredient. There can be no true success unless everyone involved with that success has won.

The 'win for all' ingredient is magic

The alternatives are *'you win and they lose'* . . . *'you lose and they win'* . . . *'you lose and they lose'* . . . *'we don't play at all'*.

Find the 'win for all' ingredient and you will have total success. In a deal, all parties will be happy. You will be able to do business again, because you took the time to find the 'win for all' magic ingredient.

Risk a bit more giving. Next time you are wondering how much to put in the box, triple what you decide.

Expect the best from life, and life will do its best to give you exactly what you have asked of it!

There is no benefit in keeping this new formula for success to yourself. Knowledge crystallises into a useless obstacle unless you allow it to flow through you and into others. You won't steal a lead on a rival by not telling him about your new-found wisdom. If you are looking at life with long-term vision, then I suggest that the only way forward is to *spread the word!*

STAGE SEVEN

Spread the word

'Now this is not the end. It is not even the beginning of the end. But it is perhaps the end of the beginning' Winston Churchill

We can't talk about success and being a good person, without touching on the subject of whatever you prefer to call the phenomenon . . . *Infinite Intelligence, the Supreme Being, Lord, Native State, the Wise One, Allah, the Divine Being, the All, the Breath, the Almighty*, or just plain old-fashioned *God*?

Whatever you believe in is healthy, as long as it provides benefit to your surroundings. If your belief is advantageous for others, then I think you will find that ultimately it has to be good for you. Other people's viewpoints can be exciting and exhilarating, but usually only if they are different from your own. A wise person listens, takes note and expands on an already existing individual outlook. Viewpoints on religion exist only because they have, or at one time did have, truth and relevance in life.

What is sacred for you can be sacred for others . . . but not necessarily. Don't force your point of view down someone else's throat without invitation, and remember as I do now, that religion can be a very tricky subject to deal with.

I believe that anything good is spiritual in its

essence, and anything bad is the opposite, with shades in between. Good and bad are harmonics of exactly the same quality, and it is a natural law of the universe that this *law of opposites* exists. It can also be illustrated with such opposites as *love and hate, fear and courage, up and down, strength and weakness* . . . the power inherent in the ability to change opposites into more beneficial harmonics is vast!

Man is basically good, and it is that quality which you should address at all times

If you appeal to the good side of a person's nature, with persistence, it will always be advantageous to both yourself and the other person.

My viewpoint on God was a personal secret for a long time. When you talk publicly about your viewpoints on God, you risk alienating certain people who ordinarily would be attracted to you. These personal views of mine are so simple and inoffensive that I now see no reason why they cannot be shared.

I believe that you are God!

I believe that I am God. I believe that a stronger God appears when you and I get together. I believe that the ultimate God is the reunification of every being back into one unit. I believe that we emanated from a whole that remained integral, without undermining our own stature of beingness.

I believe that we were as one a long time ago. We started this universe as a game . . . a game that got out of hand. We wanted something to do and we got it. We wanted a problem and we have it. We are fascinated with matter and therefore attract it. We blame others, and the ultimate irony is when we blame God without seeing ourselves as part of that equation. How many times has God's will been blamed for failure?

There exists a Quality which we call God, and from this Quality we emanate, yet that Quality still exists as a whole. God has a will, and a plan for this universe exists, but I have yet to discover anyone on earth who knows it.

There exists a consciousness where this will of God is known, and a planetary hierarchy of evolved beings who remain accountable for this planet of ours. There are beings in this world who assume massive amounts of earthly responsibility, and in this New Age of Aquarius which is dawning, higher spiritual energies are touching human consciousness. We all emanated from the same source point, and knowing this information enables you to see an enemy as a potential ally with far greater ease than if this were not so. Do not decrease your chance of success by not utilising this knowledge.

I feel that we are an important part of this universe

It thrills me when I experience the awareness of this universe flowing through me. If you embrace this viewpoint casually, even for just one minute, that the universe is the whole, and we are the cells that comprise it, then you may feel a surge of beautiful energy surround you.

You have a consciousness that is evolving just like

those from the animal and plant kingdoms. We have bodies comprising many individual cells. When a cell gets sick, or begins to behave outside its brief, the whole body can get ill. The cells can become malignant spreading growths . . . this would make them cancerous. They may have to be surgically removed, or they may kill the body that houses them before removal is possible.

We understand this process more and more each day. If we liken ourselves to a single body cell, as we can the whole body to the universe, then we can see that deviant behaviour can have tragic consequences. We are all totally interdependent, just like the cells of a human body.

A toe cell may never come into contact with a nose cell, but they still need each other. Likewise with a fellow human being in a country that you have no understanding of, and no desire to learn about . . . an interdependence still exists.

The brain cannot exist without a heart to pump around the blood, the liver and kidneys are useless without a stomach, and all of these organs are made whole from a conglomeration of single cells . . . rather like the relationship that human beings have with the universe.

We can fight other planets and destroy the universe to which we all belong. We may battle other countries and destroy a section of the planet with nuclear fallout. We can decide to enter into combat against our fellow countrymen because they live in a separate area and speak with a different accent. Do those people traditionally following different religions yet worshipping the same God as we do pose a threat?

We can fight street to street, and constantly remind ourselves of all the reasons why we should hate others, without assimilating the fact that love is a harmonic of hate which can be experienced under very similar circumstances. We can fight within our own families, and decide that we no longer love the person we pledged ourselves to for the rest of our lives. *We can fight ourselves . . . or make peace.*

We are part of the same unit and fortunate to be in possession of such knowledge. The more people we educate to an understanding of this principle, the easier and more joyful the world will become.

We have to rid ourselves of bigoted symbolism and intolerant tradition

We cannot commit crimes in the name of tradition. We can't go to war saying that God is on our side and not the other. It is just the same as the cancerous cells that eventually kill the host, and the tapeworm that destroys the environment in which it lives.

We are all microcosms of the universe

Similar patterns repeat themselves, from the universe as a whole down to the single cell. If you embrace this theory you will only know love and joy. *Hatred and sorrow cannot exist in the presence of this big picture!*

If you allow yourself the privilege of this big picture, then I guarantee you true success. Always view the whole picture. Ultimately that picture will be the universe, but can begin as something as trivial as being upset in your job because you got something wrong. See that your upset is inconsequential, as the correction that was made on your work by someone else put the firm you work for in a healthier position. *The firm is the universe.*

You may be in opposition to the political party presently governing your country, but you must acknowledge them when they do something that benefits your populace. *The country is the universe.*

You are against giving aid to the Third World because you think they should fend for themselves, then you learn that a British doctor has just saved the life of a no nothing nobody from nowhere. Feel joy . . . *both countries are the universe.*

The united cells of your body . . . the united members of your family . . . the united groups of your town . . . the united towns of your country . . . the united states of earth . . . the united planets of the universe.

Now is the time to get it together for the future. Let's get it right. We have the technology for physical abundance, and the technology of human science is understood with greater depth as each day passes. We know how to programme the subconscious mind to make it serve us. We know how to encourage ourselves into a positive and happy frame of mind. Every single step you take, no matter how small or seemingly insignificant, has to have as its basic motivation the desire to do some good.

You have read this far, and there is now no turning back. You cannot utilise the knowledge that I have shared with you successfully, without putting it to work for the good of mankind. As you serve your fellow man, then you will be rewarded with an abundance of whatever is your fancy. I have told you how to programme your SM and make it work for you. *This data was a secret of the universe until very recently.* You have to grant it this position of altitude and pledge your allegiance to the concept of the PAC. The PAC is an idea that you carry with you wherever you may travel, and a concept with which you live your life.

The basic qualification for entry to the PAC: you must believe that anything can be achieved from a positive frame of mind.

You are an Advanced PAC Practitioner and I take for granted the fact that you possess this basic requirement. The responsibility for the future of the universe now rests in your hands, and it is your job to demonstrate that we can all succeed with some basic guidance and a positive attitude. You have to teach by example. Your actions will be a direct reflection of your state of mind. You can demonstrate your intentions in very small ways to begin with; the size of your action is virtually immaterial.

One of the most thrilling experiences of my life was when I consciously chose someone whom I had not liked for some time, and who had certainly not liked me for a similar length of time, and decided to contact him and be friends. It was a simple act, but when I saw it work, it was a powerful lesson. There was no need for this contact, no ulterior motive, I just wanted to do it. Can you imagine if everyone did this even once in their lives? Can you see how much universal negativity this would rid the planet of?

You can do it. You can decide right now to make your peace with the world. To banish any anger from your life, and demand the good things that are on offer.

If you believe in mankind . . . and you should, it's here and most definitely tangible . . . then why not do this right now?

Demand the positive and banish the negative

If you ultimately believe that you are related to the rest of mankind, it makes giving to others so much easier. You are almost giving to yourself. Learn something new every day, and be willing to pass this data on for others to enjoy.

Keep positive mental images in your mind, for it is the content of your mind that will transfer itself into physical reality

Have you ever thought about someone whilst in a good mood, and remembered a time when you thought bad things about them? You feel a little embarrassed don't you? If you keep your thoughts positive, you cannot feel bad about anyone. Always look at people from a good mood perspective. When you feel bad about someone, it is you who is feeling bad. *Why punish yourself?*

This is the game we are playing. The game of life in the physical universe. Decide to live in harmony with the world that surrounds you, and get what you want from life by serving others. Get more from life by working out how you can serve your fellow man even more. *Is your cup half full or half empty?* See the best in the worst and the worst never.

Your personal success starts with you . . . here and now!

This success will be as great as you can have great thoughts. It will arrive as quickly as you are able to get into action. It will be as thorough as your plans are detailed. You will be as worthy as your outlook is on others. You will be as interesting as you are interested in others. Always listen more than you talk.

You are an Advanced PAC Practitioner! Go and succeed!

ABOUT THE PAC

If you believe that absolutely anything can be achieved from a positive frame of mind, then I invite you to join the club. You can live with the PAC as a concept only, or physically join with us. There is no other qualification whatsoever!

I hope that people from all walks of life and educational backgrounds who embrace this philosophy, will join forces and share energies. Together we can blaze a trail, whilst planning a healthy and prosperous future. We can serve ourselves by serving the world and individual alike.

Through the PAC, we can share our knowledge of the positive.

There are books, cassettes and videos available, that can help form the basis of any positive plans you may have for your future. In addition to existing programmes, there is new material being written every day to help those who help themselves. I promise that the PAC will keep abreast of all data concerning the philosophy of positive attitude, and make it available to members. That will be a pleasure!

The PAC will become an action station for the furtherance of positive attitudes throughout the world. Read the PAC Mission Statement, and if you like what you see, and feel that you can win by subscribing to this idea . . . join the PAC. Do it now without procrastination . . . today!

I look forward to us sharing a wonderful future together . . .

With love,
Phil Murray
Leader of the PAC

The PAC Mission Statement

Through dissemination of quality spiritual and worldly material, living the talk and enjoying the Path of Transformation, we aim to render whatever assistance is required for The Journey.

Ultimate Goal: Premier State.

The PAC philosophy

The improvement of personal life through positive attitudes benefits mankind as a whole.

Visualisation Statement

1. A large and increasing membership.
2. We aid members' awareness of positive reading, writing and viewing materials.
3. We help the world, with a constant output of positive affirmations from all members.
4. We influence the world for the better in every way, shape and form.

5. We show by example that the PAC philosophy works.
6. We influence the media and world governments, by living the talk of our philosophy.
7. We exist wherever there are people who can benefit and prosper from PAC principles.
8. We are revered as an organisation of high principle, honour and integrity.
9. We are available for consultation concerning disagreements between peoples of the world, with the aim of solving all problems on a 'win for all' basis.
10. Happiness during the Return Journey.

Phil Murray
Leader of the PAC, 1st January 1997

FEELING GOOD ABOUT YOURSELF HAS A POSITIVE IMPACT
ON EVERYONE AND EVERYTHING AROUND YOU

The Positive Attitude Club

Madeira, Hunts Road, St Lawrence, Isle of Wight PO38 1XT, England

E MAIL: 101376.154@COMPUSERVE.COM

http://ourworld.compuserve.com/homepages/Phil_Murray_7

WELCOME TO THE CONSTANTLY EVOLVING PAC CONCEPT
The Positive Attitude Club accepts applications from anyone wishing
to join in with the spirit of the idea. All we ask is that they
embrace the philosophy that positive attitudes are helpful. This
is a members' organisation; direction, activities and content ideas
are always welcome. In line with our plans for the expansion of
this beautifully simple philosophy, every member is invited to begin
their own local PAC along the lines of *forward thinking through creative
discussion*. In harmony with my own Mission Statement, I shall be
available for as many activities as are practical to my own schedule.
Large or small, old or young . . . all becomes irrelevant when immersed
in inspirational interdependence!

Name ....

Address ....

....

.... Postcode ....

Telephone ....

Occupation ....

Contribution ....
towards seasonal newsletter, meeting costs and general administration

Membership Number ..... *to be allotted* .....

Let's enjoy today, and look forward to a rosy future together.

Phil Murray
Leader of the PAC, 1st January 1997

PAC is an acronym for Positive Attitude Club.
The PAC philosophy states simply that improvement of personal life
through positive attitudes benefits humanity as a whole.
We are an independent non-profit-making organisation dedicated to peaceful
interdependence through creative discussion and forward thinking for the world.

BIBLIOGRAPHY

Suggested further reading and listening

As a Man Thinketh (Book and Audio Programme),
  James Allen
The books by *Alice A Bailey*
The books by *H P Blavatsky*
How to Win Friends and Influence People, *Dale Carnegie*
The Richest Man In Babylon, *George S Clason*
The 7 Habits of Highly Effective People, *Dr Stephen
  R Covey*
Principle Centred Leadership (Audio Cassette), *Dr
  Stephen R Covey*
You'll See it When You Believe it, *Dr Wayne W
  Dyer*
Creative Visualization, *Shakti Gawain*
What To Say When You Talk To Yourself, *Shad
  Helmstetter*
The Science of Personal Achievement (Audio Programme),
  Napoleon Hill
Think and Grow Rich, *Napoleon Hill*
Success Through a Positive Mental Attitude, *Napoleon
  Hill and W Clement Stone*
Swim With the Sharks Without Being Eaten Alive,
  Harvey Mackay
Psycho-Cybernetics, *Maxwell Maltz*
Before The Beginning Is A Thought (Book and Audio
  Programme), *Phil Murray*
Bites (Book and Audio Programmes), *Phil Murray*
Empowerment (Book and Audio Programmes),
  Phil Murray

The 49 Steps (Book and Audio Programmes), *Phil Murray*

You Can Always Get What You Want (Book and Audio Programmes), *Phil Murray*

NLP: The New Technology Of Achievement (Audio Programme), *NLP Comprehensive*

Awaken the Giant Within, *Anthony Robbins*

Accelerated Learning, *Colin Rose*

Doorways (Audio Cassette), *Nico Thelman*

Memories (Audio Cassette), *Nico Thelman*

The Plan (Audio Cassette), *Nico Thelman*

Maximum Achievement, *Brian Tracy*

The Psychology of Achievement (Audio Programme), *Brian Tracy*

Seeds of Greatness, *Dennis Waitley*